THE
LIFE
OF
Chandra

T. PELLETIER

Fulton Books, Inc.
Meadville, PA

Published by Fulton Books 2021

ISBN 978-1-63860-132-6 (paperback)
ISBN 978-1-63860-133-3 (digital)

Printed in the United States of America

She awoke confused. A little warm and disoriented from too many people being in the bed. She couldn't understand what was going on next to her. Later, she would learn that it was her mother and sister's father having sex. Maybe that was the night her sister was conceived. Chandra was four years old, living with a house full of people. She was living with her mom, Clarissa, Granny Ann, Uncle Joseph, and Grandpa John. She was, at this time, the baby of the family and adored by all. Her innocence and joy were something to be admired by all around her. Clarissa was only sixteen when she found out she was pregnant with Chandra. She knew that she would be graduating with broken ambitions. She had dreamed of going to the Air Force, but now she would find a different path to be able to provide for herself and her child. Granny Ann felt that if Clarissa wanted to play grown up and have a baby, she would have to stay and take care of the baby. Clarissa was in love with just being in love. She didn't really know what love was, but her version was real to her. If a man paid any attention to her and told her sweet things, he must have loved her.

Chandra's father, Bill, had broken her heart when he decided to leave her and Chandra behind for someone new. He even went as far as bringing his new love to the hospital when Clarissa was giving birth. It was hard enough for her, knowing that he had moved on, but to flaunt his new love interest in her face made the pain more real. He maintained distance and never wavered from the fact that he wanted nothing to do with neither Clarissa nor Chandra. Bill was year younger than Clarissa, so he didn't graduate until Chandra was four months old. It was at that time he decided to join the military and completely leave Chandra and Clarissa behind. Bill had two sisters, his mom, and his dad. Only one sister and Bill's parents ever acknowledge Chandra's existence. Even when he was serving the country overseas, his parents and his sister maintained contact with Clarissa and Chandra.

Clarissa eventually moved on to a new love in her life named Chad. This was where Chandra's life journey began. Chad was very handsome to many women in town. He also was available to many women in town. Chad was good at playing the field and breaking hearts. He was six feet tall four inches. He had the most beautiful green eyes and dark skin that was flawless. He had a build of an athlete and knew how to wear his confidence well. Clarissa thought she had met the man of her dreams. It was confirmed by the mere fact that he paid attention to her.

Chad would buy her flowers and take her out on dates and show her off to his family and friends. She knew more than anything she wanted him to be her future husband. He was handsome, rich, he loved kids; and most of all, he loved and doted over Chandra. He was the absolute perfect man until he started drinking. Chad had a horrible drinking habit that made him turn abusive. Clarissa thought for the longest time it was the drinking that would bring on the abusive behavior but later learned that hitting women was just his character. He began beating Clarissa daily. She endured the beatings and hid the bruises and the pain from everyone around her because of how good Chad treated Chandra. Chandra, at the time, was his most valuable possession.

Although biologically she wasn't his child, he loved her unconditionally. Eventually, in between beatings, Clarissa became pregnant. When she gained the courage to tell Chad, he seemed to be the happiest man in the world. Clarissa's beatings were nonexistent while she was carrying his seed. He was loving, attentive, and almost unrecognizable to her. Her pregnancy brought joy and almost a family feel to them. Clarissa ended up having an amazing pregnancy filled with excitement, enthusiasm, and completion. She didn't experience sickness as she had with Chandra.

She also had a man that stood by her side throughout her pregnancy. His family was also wonderful in the support they showed as well. She ended up having successful delivery. Clarissa gave birth to a beautiful baby girl named Aria. She was the splitting image of her dad. She was absolutely gorgeous. She had the most beautiful green eyes like her dad, his silky black hair, but her mother's olive skin. She was the picture of perfection to all who saw her. Immediately, everyone around her fell in love with her. Chandra was obsessed with her baby sister. Finally, she was here in the flesh. Chandra knew they would eventually become the best of friends.

Joy, however, was short-lived. Clarissa was made to remain in the hospital for five days due to Aria's blood disease. It was a hereditary disease that the doctor wanted to make sure Clarissa was aware of and that she knew the challenges that she would face. Chandra was made to stay at the family home in the care of her grandmother. On the third day of Clarissa and Aria's stay at the hospital, a very attractive doctor was on staff tending to Clarissa. This did not sit well with Chad at all. The doctor on staff had visited Clarissa's room while Chad was out getting some lunch.

When Chad returned to the room, he passed the doctor on his way exiting the room. He immediately became enraged. There was no time for Clarissa to think about a plan of action. Chad began asking or interrogating Clarissa about her relationship with the doctor. She spoke quietly to Chad in hopes that this would diminish his anger. To no avail, Chad lost control. He began beating on Clarissa in the hospital room while she lay in the hospital bed. Nurses heard the commotion and cries and rushed in to check on Clarissa. To their shock and dismay, Chad had beaten her relentlessly. He was restrained by nurses and staff until the proper authorities came and took him away. There was blood everywhere. Clarissa chose not to press charges, and to maintain the lie that she had fallen on the floor and hit her face on the wheels of the bed.

There was nothing anyone could do at that point. However, the beating was the final straw for Clarissa. She could take the cheating and verbal abuse, but she wasn't willing to go back to the physical beatings from Chad. After being released from the hospital, she chose to only allow Chad to see the kids through her mom. And never come into contact with her again. He was in and out of Chandra and Aria's life after that day. Chad's family took over and played a consistent part in both Chandra and Aria's life. They would call, come see them, and make sure the girls had any and everything they needed. Clarissa knew that she needed some finality in her relationship with Chad and wanted things to be clarified as far as visits and custody went. She hadn't seen Chad in some months, and he had been adhering to the rules of picking up the girls and seeing the girls through contact with her mom. So she thought the two of them could sit down and handle things like adults for once and for all. She called Chad over for a face-to-face conversation. Knowing that her brother would be home at the time of their discussion, Clarissa had no fear in what Chad would do.

Chad readily agreed to come over and have a conversation with Clarissa, thinking maybe they would discuss reconciliation. When he arrived, he was highly disappointed with the custody papers that Clarissa presented to him. Clarissa began to see the anger creep up on Chad's face. His voice was low, and his eyes were fuming. She had seen this look before and knew that she had made the right decision of leaving the girls in the playroom watching cartoons. Chad punched Clarissa so hard, she immediately fell on the floor. As he was pounding her frail body, Joseph, Clarissa's brother, walked in the room. Chandra followed him in as well. Joseph pulled Chad off Clarissa and began giving him the beating he deserved. Chandra didn't understand what was going on at all. She knew in heart that what was going on was bad and wanted to help her uncle, so she began to bite Chad while Joseph had him on the ground, pounding him.

Noticing what was going on around her, Clarissa was conscious enough to pull Chandra out of the way of danger. When Joseph realized the tears and cries of Clarissa and Chandra, he stopped the beating and allowed Chad to get up. Chad was allowed to go to the restroom to clean off his face. Joseph told Chad to leave and never return to their home. Clarissa, knowing the love the girls had for Chad and the love he had for them, was unwilling to cut off their communication at its entirety. It was made clear that he would only have visits with her children in the presence of his family. He was never allowed with the girls alone. There was also an agreement that there would be no overnight visits. Chandra was five years old at this time and had already witnessed too much for a child her age. Witnessing this much pain and abuse had already left a mark on her heart that would later need mending. Chandra knew love from a man as pain.

It had been seven months since the incident with Chad. Clarissa and the girls were happily moving on. The girls were growing and learning in ways that shocked even Clarissa. Clarissa was secretly seeing a new man in her life and was reluctant about introducing him to her children. She had made a vow to herself that her kids would never see her hurt again. As unrealistic as she knew that vow was, she was still trying to make sure the girls remained safe from her love life. She wanted to make sure that she didn't rush into anything too soon.

Clarissa had met a man named Ray. She contemplated over how long she should know and date him before introducing him to her girls. They had been secretly seeing each other for six months. She thought to herself that it would be a good time for her girls to meet him. So one day, Clarissa took the girls to Pizza Hut for lunch, but in reality, it was so Ray could come and meet them in a neutral location. She knew that her mom would not approve of her introducing a new man into the girls' lives so quickly. Immediately, Chandra knew Ray had something very off about him. Chandra was not comfortable around him from the very beginning. She had a genuine fear of him from the start. It was something in his eyes. She wouldn't even attempt to go near him. Aria, on the other hand, was always friendly to anyone she met. She immediately reached out to Ray as if she knew him her entire life. Aria was an arm baby. She simply loved to be held. Aria was only a year old and absolutely loved to be held. Clarissa always joked that Ray was Aria's replacement dad.

Clarissa thought it was time to introduce Ray to the remainder of the family. It would be the first time he visited their home. Chandra never seemed to warm up to Ray, at any time, during his and Clarissa's courtship. Ray never tried to force it either. He would spend the time with Aria and tell Clarissa that Chandra would come around eventually. He always seemed to play down the situation between he and Chandra. Now that Ray was allowed to come to the house more often, Clarissa thought it was time that he try to reach out for Chandra. When he did, Chandra would always run away and stay in the presence of her granny or uncle. There was always an uneasy feeling between the two. Eventually, Ray became a constant in the home, and everyone became comfortable having him around. Chandra was still standoffish, but she was at least polite and began to be kind to him. He was, in fact, winning her over.

Granny Ann, Grandpa John, and Uncle Joseph decided to go on vacation for the weekend. This was the first vacation that Clarissa wouldn't allow the baby girls to go on. She felt that she was in a place in her life where she could keep the girls alone. She also figured it was the most perfect time to throw a house party. It had been a while since she was able to fully enjoy herself and hang out with friends. Granny Ann always gave her a time to come home to the girls. She felt that she needed some party time with her girls. Now, with everyone gone, she could put the girls to bed and simply enjoy her night. She wanted her friends to be introduced to the new love in her as well. She thought of him as her best-kept secret. Because he didn't grow up in the same town as her and her friends, no one really knew him or had heard anything about him. He was currently the man of her dreams. She had no idea of the ensuing nightmare to come.

The party planning was easy. She made a few phone calls, picked up some snacks, and got together the right music. No turning back. All her friends showed up and had a ball. They laughed, played games, and simply reminisced over old times. During the party, Clarissa let herself relax a little too much and took one too many shots. She began slurring words and eventually found herself asleep on the couch. Her friends eventually all went home. Ray decided he would be the sober one of the night so that Clarissa could have some much-needed fun. He felt that she deserved to let her hair down for once. He allowed her to have herself a much-needed good time with her friends, and he told her that he would keep his eyes and ears open for the girls. She had no fear of any danger in the situation, knowing that she would be in the house the entire time. She felt the girls would be safe as long as she was there physically.

After all the guest had exited the house and were in their cars, Ray went inside to check on Clarissa. She was out cold on the couch.

He began to clean up the empty beer cans and paper plates and cups that were left in the living. As he was taking the trash into the kitchen, he thought he heard crying in the girls' bedroom. He tiptoed down the hall closer to the door and could hear Chandra's small voice calling out for her Granny Ann. Chandra was used to calling on her granny or her uncle in the middle of the night and not her mom.

When Aria was born, Granny Ann built an addition to the house on the other side so that Clarissa could have some privacy. She kept Chandra's room on the same side of the house as hers. So Chandra was used to calling on Granny Ann and not Clarissa. Ray doubled back to ensure Clarissa was indeed still passed out. He crept into the girls' room and told Chandra it was okay and to settle down because her mom was asleep. Chandra was fearful because she still didn't trust Ray. She could tell that he was very annoyed at her mere existence. He was also annoyed that she was awake and crying. Exiting the room, Ray noticed the iron plugged in and left on inside the room. He walked backed in and unplugged the iron and began to wrap the cord around the bottom. As he began to walk the iron out of the room, he walked over to Chandra and stuck the hot side of the iron on her arm causing her to scream a gut-wrenching scream. Her scream was so loud, it was felt in Clarissa's soul because she woke up and came running.

Ray immediately went into action as a caring boyfriend. He grabbed Chandra and acted as if he was rescuing her from her careless actions. Clarissa, being drunk, wasn't fully aware of what was going on around her. She was trying to process her daughter being hurt, and how much damage could have done with the iron. She grabbed Chandra from Ray and took her to run cold water on the burn. She added Vaseline and a bandage. She eventually calmed Chandra down enough to ask her what happened. Even at her tender age of six, Chandra knew that she had to lie. Clarissa then began to fuss at Chandra in anger and out of fear of what could have happened. Ray lied about running in there and saving Chandra from the hot iron, and the pain she could have caused herself. He pretended that he was her hero. He played the part very well.

That night, fear was birthed in the heart of Chandra. She knew that if he wanted, Ray would hurt her and probably get away with it. As time went on, things began to escalate, and Chandra was in fear more and more. He would do subtle things like trip her when no one was looking. He would pinch her until she would cry. She knew she was never safe when he was around. Her fear was always that no one would believe her if she did find the courage to tell. This was her life, and she had to live it. Ray's persona around others was gentle, kind, patient, and loving. Chandra knew that this would make everyone question if she said otherwise. Clarissa was in love and living on cloud nine. Aria was too small to care, and Chandra was walking in hell and couldn't find any peace. Ray's family didn't make things any better. Jealousy of the love Ray showed, Clarissa made them hate Chandra as well. They treated her as a maid when they would come around. When Clarissa would make Chandra go with them on vacation, she was made to do all the work while the other kids played. She was the oldest and was expected to watch the others.

A year had gone by since the incident. Chandra was now seven years old. She was no longer that joyful little girl that everyone doted over. She had become quiet and withdrawn. The world was eating her alive, and she was screaming, but no one could hear her. Aria had many aches and pains within the last two years due to her blood disease, so the focus was on her. This made it easier for Chandra to be overlooked. Chandra often tried to hide away. Granny Ann and Grandpa John would take most of their time with Aria, and this left Chandra to endure time spent with Ray and his family. Chandra hated feeling like the outcast, but she knew that she had to keep quiet and keep her mom happy. That was her job.

One night, Aria began crying uncontrollably. Clarissa knew that she had no other choice but to take her to the emergency room. Her mother, stepfather, and brother were all away from the house at the time. She was uncomfortable in her decision, but she had no other choice but to leave Chandra in the care of Ray alone. She had never left him or any man alone with her daughter before. She put Chandra to bed and asked her to stay in bed until she returned. Chandra was very afraid. She knew that this would be the perfect time for Ray to hit her or burn her or cause some type of pain to her. She knew that she wasn't liked by Ray at all. She wanted to scream and cry and tell her mom something, but her love for Aria allowed her to remain quiet and calm. She hugged her mother and promised not to move from her bed until she returned. She gave Aria a kiss and comforted her as they were heading out of the room.

While lying in bed, Chandra could hear her mother and Ray talking. Her mother was getting all the items ready to take Aria to the hospital. After a short while, Chandra heard the front door close and tried her best to pretend to be asleep. She felt if she pretended to be asleep, Ray wouldn't bother her. This was the furthest thing from the truth. Ray slowly entered Chandra's bedroom. This time he was different. As he approached the bed, he was being awkwardly kind to Chandra. He rubbed her head gently and also kissed her forehead. It was as if he was trying to be a father figure and comfort her fears. Chandra opened her eyes to look at Ray. He kindly asked her how she was doing. Chandra felt as if maybe he was trying to finally be nice to her. Ray offered her some special water that would make all her worries go away. Chandra drank the water even though it was the nastiest thing she had ever tasted. She didn't want him to get angry at her. The water made her very tired.

She asked Ray if she could go to sleep. He told her that since he had shared his special water with her, she was obligated to be special to him. This would be the very first time Ray would rape Chandra. Chandra knew that it was wrong. No man should touch a girl in this way. The pain was unbearable. Chandra decided to pretend to be somewhere else. In her head, she started replaying cartoons that she had recently seen. She started singing songs. She had never gone through this before and didn't know how long it was going to last. She could smell the cigarette smoke coming off of Ray's body. It was the most disgusting smell she had ever smelled. His hair reeked of jerry curl. It was wet and sticky. He was heavy, so very heavy. Chandra just wanted it to be over. When he was done, he made Chandra get up and take the rest of her clothes off. There was blood, so much blood. He made Chandra get in a bath that he had run for her and began doing laundry.

When Clarissa returned home with Aria, she was exhausted from having to sit at the hospital. All she wanted to do was put Aria to bed and take a shower. When she walked inside the house, she noticed Ray doing laundry. This was odd to her. She went directly into Chandra's room to check on her as she lay Aria down in the bed beside hers. She was frightened to find Chandra not in her bed. She also noticed that all of Chandra's bed linen was missing off her bed as well. She tucked Aria inside her bed and began searching for Ray. She walked into the laundry room, and he wasn't there. She went inside the restroom and found Ray and Chandra. Chandra was sitting in the tub with tears streaming down her face. This brought so many questions to Clarissa's mind.

She asked Ray, "What the hell is going on?"

To which he replied, "Chandra was worried about Aria, and I guess this made her pee in the bed. I gave her a good talking to and put her in the bath and her sheets in the washer."

This made Clarissa felt good inside, to think that her man cared for her child in that way. Clarissa walked over to Chandra and kneeled down to talk to her. She told Chandra that Aria was just fine, and she could stop crying. Chandra only nodded her head and asked if she could go to bed. Clarissa asked Ray to get her a towel, and she gave it to Chandra to get out of the tub and dry herself off. When Chandra was tucked into her clean bed, Clarissa talked to Ray and told him that Chandra was old enough to go in the bath alone, and the next time, he didn't need to go in there with her. He agreed, and they ended up sitting on the couch and falling asleep to the television. Granny Ann and Grandpa John were taking frequent trips away for his business, and this left Ray watching Chandra more often that she would have liked. Some of the time, she was allowed to stay with some of her cousins, but they were all in sports. And her aunts and uncles were always busy. Ray took advantage of every opportunity that he had with Chandra. Some days when he would have to babysit, he would make Chandra drink alcohol to calm her down. And other days, he would give her chewing tobacco. The tobacco would often make her sick. Chandra had learned to take her mind to other places. She knew the pain would come, and she had learned to endure it. Over the next few years, she even learned not to cry.

It had been two years now, and Chandra was nine years old. Chandra and Aria were the best of friends. Aria wanted to be everywhere Chandra was. Aria would never understand or begin to comprehend the love Chandra had for her. Chandra was her protector and would do anything in the world to keep Aria away from harm. She shielded Aria from the pains and the evils of their world. Granny Ann was now at home more than she was away. She was constant in the girls' lives. During this time, Chandra was awarded a sense of security having them all home. Ray was still Chandra's nightmare, and every chance that was made available to him, he would take and rape Chandra. The abuse, sometimes, was worse than the rape because the bruises were getting harder to hide. Chandra was numb inside. To protect Aria, Chandra was willing to take whatever Ray had wanted to offer. His new threat was to threaten her sister. He knew how to manipulate Chandra all too well. She would give everything of herself to keep her sister at peace. Chandra knew that Aria could not withstand the pain that she was going through. The beatings alone would send Aria to the hospital.

One very hot day during that summer, Clarissa called a family meeting. This brought fear to Chandra because she thought that maybe her mom had found out about her and Ray and would blame her for it all. Ray was invited to this meeting, so she knew that it couldn't be anything good. Clarissa and Ray were standing in the front of the living room together as the family started sitting in the couches around them. Granny Ann, Grandpa John, and Uncle Joseph sat on the couches and sat Aria and Chandra on their laps.

Ray began to smile and started to speak, "My beautiful lady and I feel as if it is time we move into a house of our own."

During this time, Chandra's heart began to sink, and the tears were fighting for their escape. She knew that if even one tear dropped, it would mean her demise later.

He continued, "We have also decided that our daughters would be coming with us into our new home."

Inside, Chandra screamed, "Daughters, who is your daughter?"

Unknowingly, Chandra was squeezing Granny Ann's hand extremely hard. When she realized, she immediately withdrew her hand. Chandra prayed that it wasn't noticed by Ray or Granny Ann. With all the commotion that was now going around the room, Chandra felt safe and that she had gotten away with that slipup. Everyone was talking amongst themselves and looking at pictures of the house they would be moving into. Granny Ann, however, was not thinking of looking at the pictures at all. She had other things on her mind. Chandra had, in fact, not gotten away with the hand squeeze at all. Granny Ann walked Chandra to her room and sat her down on her bed.

"Baby girl, is there anything you want granny to know?"

Chandra was terrified and shook her head no. This could mean that Aria would be put in danger. She knew not to speak a word. How could she tell her granny what was going on? Clearly after allowing him to do this for so long, it had to be her fault. It was definitely her fault that it was still happening. She doesn't say no. She continued to go along with it. Keeping everyone safe had to be a good enough reason to keep this secret, right? Granny Ann just stood there; she absolutely knew in her heart that her baby was holding onto something but wasn't going to push her to reveal it until she was ready. She sat and held Chandra in her arms knowing that her baby was fighting a demon that she couldn't place her hand on. She and Chandra eventually made their way back into the living room and the celebration.

Granny Ann had a horrible feeling in the pit of her stomach and prayed continuously that whatever was going on was eventually revealed. The next seven months seemed to go by way too fast for Chandra. The closer they got to moving out, the worse the beatings were. Ray would wait until everyone was asleep and pretend to catch Chandra doing various things just to spank her. On the nights that Clarissa would sneak him in to spend the night, he would make his way to Chandra's room in the dead of night and mess with her. Chandra never made a sound. She knew better. She always prayed that someone would wake up and catch them. It never happened. Chandra always thought that because she continued to let these things happen, God had truly forgotten who she was.

It took about seven months for the house to be fully built and ready to be lived in. Moving day was finally here. Ray and Clarissa were ecstatic. Aria couldn't comprehend what was happening, she only knew that she was getting her own room and that she would have a Care Bear night light. Chandra was eerily quiet the entire day. The families of Clarissa and Ray were all too eager to help them move into their new home. The families stayed for dinner, and Aria and Chandra went to Granny Ann's for the night. The furniture for their bedrooms would not be bought until the following day. The following day came, and Clarissa asked Granny Ann to go with her to the store and that Ray would watch the girls. Aria was in the room asleep, and Chandra was in the room reading her books. So Granny Ann didn't see anything wrong with that. She knew that Uncle Joseph would be coming home within a few hours, and Ray wouldn't have to babysit for long. Granny Ann was uneasy, but she reminded Ray that Joseph would be there within an hour to get the girls and that he didn't have to even go in the bedrooms to check on them unless they came out. The two women left to buy the girls their bedroom sets.

Ray immediately ran in the room with Chandra and asked her what she had told her Granny Ann about them. Chandra denied saying anything, and Ray went to walk out of the room. As he reached the door, he picked up an item on the dresser and threw it into Chandra's tummy. She fell to the floor, and he told her they didn't have much time. He proceeded to rape her. Granny Ann and Clarissa were out no more than two hours. It only took that long because Clarissa couldn't make up her mind what type of beds she wanted for the girls' rooms. When they returned, Granny Ann immediately went to check on Chandra and Aria. Aria was sitting on the floor watching television, and Chandra was in the bed complaining of a tummy ache. Uncle Joseph still hadn't return from the errands he was running earlier. Granny Ann was sure he must have stopped at a friend's house or something. Granny Ann kept asking Chandra if she was okay, and she was saying her tummy ached and that is all that she would say.

Granny Ann felt uneasy seeing as Ray told her Chandra hadn't complained to him the entire time that he was watching them.

Eventually, Granny Ann gave in and let it go. She gave Chandra some Tylenol and told Clarissa and Ray that she would keep the girls another night, so they could enjoy themselves and get some things unpacked in peace. Oddly enough, Ray seemed to disagree with the girls staying at their Granny Ann's house. Granny Ann didn't like his demeanor at all. She insisted and dang near demanded Clarissa to allow the girls to stay at her place and get a good night's sleep. Ray's behavior raised some red flags and concerns, and Granny Ann was determined to find some truth. She didn't trust the words of her granddaughter when she stated that everything was okay and began watching her every move. The next morning when Chandra was in the shower, Granny Ann noticed the blood-stained sheets that were left on Chandra's bed. Chandra explained she had cut herself while wiping and that also didn't sit well with her grandma. Granny Ann went to her room and began to pray. She knew that something was going on with her baby, but she couldn't get it out of her. She didn't want to assume and jump to conclusions, but she knew and she could only pray that God would wrap his arms around her and protect her.

On Chandra's tenth birthday, she was given a party by Clarissa and had a few of her class friends over for cake and ice cream. A few boys from the neighborhood joined as well. All the kids were laughing and having a great time. One of the neighborhood boys joked around saying that Chandra was his girlfriend. This made Ray very angry. Chandra could see steam coming from his head. She could feel the anger coming out of his skin. She knew in her heart that she would be punished when everyone would leave. Chandra decided to enjoy herself while she could. All her friends began to leave the party, and a few of her girlfriends asked to have a sleepover. Clarissa couldn't allow them to stay because she had to work the night shift that night.

When Clarissa went to work that night, Ray decided to take things up a notch with Chandra and made her perform oral sex and raped her repeatedly because she was being a whore by inviting boys to her party. During all this time, Chandra knew that she was protecting Aria, and as long as she fulfilled his every desire, he would not touch her sister. Her love for Aria was unconditional. Aria was indeed the center of her heart and her only joy. This was her normal. There were no tears left to cry. She was dead, completely dead inside. She felt no pain, no shame, and no feelings at all. She couldn't be saved. There was nothing or no one in this world that could save her.

Things were really getting bad for her before her mom said yes to his marriage proposal. The first time Ray proposed, Clarissa said she wasn't ready for that type of commitment, and Chandra paid the price that night by being raped by him three times in one night. He made her do things that no child would ever dream up. Her body was his trash can, and he usually made daily deposits. To her relief, Clarissa finally said yes, and Ray let up just a little bit on Chandra. His mom was starting to visit more as well. She would stay over well into the night hours. When she would finally leave, Ray would sometimes be too tired to bother Chandra. The wedding day was quickly approaching, and things were too hectic lately for Ray to bother Chandra.

Two days before the wedding, and Granny Ann fell ill. The doctors thought it was best to admit her for observation. Chandra knew that with Granny Ann in the hospital, Ray would be the one left to babysit her and her sister Aria. For the first time, she wasn't afraid. He was about to marry her mother. No way would he hurt his soon-to-be daughter. That night as Clarissa began to get ready for work, Chandra gave her a big hug and went to her bedroom. There were no tears and no fear. Chandra climbed into bed next to Aria. She usually slept with Aria on the nights their mother had to work. Aria was so energetic and happy; she was everything Chandra was before coming into contact with Ray. Chandra wrapped her arms around Aria as to protect her from any harm that may have come her way. It was around 3:00 a.m., and Chandra was awakened by a tap on her shoulder. She felt the familiar ache in the pit of her tummy. She was sick and immediately began to cry. She wasn't crying out of fear, she wasn't even crying out of sadness. She was crying out of disbelief.

This can't be happening, she thought to herself.

She then heard a comforting voice asked, "Baby girl, why are you crying?"

It was her mother, Clarissa. Chandra jumped and turned around to the best hug she had ever received. She replied to her mother, "I just missed you so much, Mom."

She wanted in that moment so desperately to tell her mom the truth of all that had transpired over the years.

It is the day of the wedding. Chandra is now ten years old. She had become very good at hiding her pain. Chandra had prayed that once Ray was officially married to her mom, he would abandon any sexual desire he had for her. Ray was very happy that she finally said yes. Chandra was happy as well. Granny Ann was released from the hospital. Everyone was getting their Sunday best together. Family from all over were arriving at the church. The wedding would begin at 1:00 p.m. Aria was the most beautiful flower girl the world had ever seen. Chandra was allowed to walk down the aisle as a mini bride. Both girls were dressed in white with dark blue bows on their gowns and in their hair.

Granny Ann decided to go with a simple blue gown that hugged her body to show that she still had the body of a goddess. The brides-maids were dressed in the most elegant blue gowns that matched the white suits and blue bow ties the groomsman wore. It was a wedding made for television for sure. It should have been; it was expensive enough. Clarissa showed up to the steps of the church carried by a horse and carriage. Her hair was hanging to the middle of her back with the top pinned up in a bun. She was absolutely stunning. As a family friend sang a song by Luther Vandrose while Clarissa walked down the aisle, family and friends stood in awe of her beauty and poise. Grandpa Dan, Clarissa's biological father, walked her down the aisle, and Grandpa John and Grandpa Dan both gave her away. After the wedding, Clarissa and Ray went to Hawaii for two weeks. This was the best two weeks of Chandra's life.

There was only two weeks left of school. Chandra was looking forward to summer break because she knew this meant she would be over Granny Ann's all the time. It had been over a month, and she hadn't been touched or even looked at by Ray. She was having the time of her life. She was finally starting to feel like a normal child again. She almost thought it was okay to smile. The sun was shining on her life, and she wanted nothing more than this feeling to last a lifetime.

It had been years since the last time Aria was bothered with bone pain. This one was a bad one. Aria was crying uncontrollably, and Granny Ann knew she had to get her to the hospital quick. Granny Ann still had no trust for Ray, so she decided to take Chandra with her and Grandpa John to the hospital with Aria. This was a relief to Chandra, although Ray hadn't bothered her in months now. As Chandra sat in the waiting room with Grandpa John, she could hear her mom, and the doctors talked with Granny Ann and Clarissa. They would be admitting Aria for blood work and magnesium. This seemed to be something of a relief to Granny Ann and Clarissa, so Chandra knew it couldn't be anything too bad. Aria would be okay. Granny Ann decided to stay the first night at the hospital with Aria which meant Chandra would be left in the care of Ray. Although Ray had not been a threat lately, Chandra still didn't want to be left alone with him.

Chandra and Clarissa arrived home to find Ray sitting in the living room with two of his friends. They were all having beers and smoking cigars. It smelled awful. Clarissa called Ray into the bedroom, and you could hear them argue throughout the house. Chandra went to her bedroom and closed the door. Clarissa was working night shift at the hospital and had to be into work in a few hours. She made sure that Chandra had her clothes for the next day out and ready and that she was in bed, and she stressed *no television*. Chandra gave her mom a kiss and drifted off to sleep. The next morning came, Chandra woke up and got ready, as instructed by her mother, and waited patiently for her mom to arrive from work. She knew not to check to see if anyone was home. She didn't want to bother Ray and didn't want him to bother her. To her surprise when her mom arrived home, she was furious. Ray had left Chandra home alone all night long and went out with his friends and still hadn't returned. This was not bad news to Chandra at all. She was so happy she was left alone.

The arguments became more frequent between Clarissa and Ray. Ray began not paying bills and was always drinking, going out, and having friends over. They would constantly be at each other's throats. Granny Ann and Grandpa John were making occasional trips out of town and every time they went, they would take Aria. Due to her blood condition, she was mainly homeschooled. It was a Friday night, and Aria happened to be home with Chandra, and they were watching television. Clarissa was called into work unexpectedly. Ray was in the living room drinking with friends as usual. Clarissa began fussing about the light bill being due and started getting ready for her shift. She called Granny Ann to come and grab the kids, but they had gone out of town for the weekend thinking that Clarissa had a few days off.

She told them not to worry about it, and let Ray know the girls would be home with him that night. He agreed, and Clarissa walked out of the door. Chandra put Aria to bed and climbed into bed herself. A few hours later, Ray came into Chandra's room. It had been so long; Chandra no longer feared him and had a false sense of security while being home alone with him. She had placed Aria in her own room that night thinking she would be safe. Ray pulled Chandra on the floor and raped her. She drifted off in the made-up world in her head that helped her block out what was going on. She knew that if he was on her, he wouldn't be on Aria. The pain was almost unbearable, but she knew she had no choice. When he was done, Chandra tried to get up and get dressed, but a few moments later, one of Ray's friends came in the room. Chandra began to cry.

Ray said, "It's either you or your sister."

Chandra knew this was the truth, and she couldn't stand the thought of this happening to Aria. She laid there, and she took it. Chandra had a way of pretending in her head that she was somewhere else in the world. When his friend was done, Ray told Chandra to roll over to her knees, and the second friend took her from behind. Chandra let out a cry that must have woken Aria because the next thing she heard was Aria asking, "What are you doing to my sister?"

All the men left the room, and Ray took Aria back to bed and told her she was dreaming. Aria insisted that she wasn't, and she knew what she saw, but Ray convinced her otherwise. Chandra was spent. She was on the floor unable to move. Her body was in so much pain. She had never felt this type of pain before. She closed her eyes and drifted off to sleep. She might have even passed out at one point. The stench of alcohol and cigars lingered in Chandra's room. A part of her wanted Clarissa to smell it and ask questions, but Chandra knew that wouldn't happen. The next day as she was sitting in her room reading her books, Chandra looked up to see Ray standing in her doorway. He looked at her and said, "Thank you for making enough money to pay the light bill."

Chandra simply went back to reading pretending that all was well. By this time in her life, pretending was one thing she was very good at doing. Her pain was constant. She didn't know how to let it out. All she knew is that she had to protect her sister from this monster. She also feared for her mom because Ray told her that if her mom ever found out, she would kick Chandra out of the house because of the heartache that she caused. Ray convinced Chandra that all was her fault and that no one would take her side. Ray had a new side hustle and that was Chandra. When a bill was due, he would find a way to make the payment by using Chandra's body with his friends. She never complained and never told a soul. She knew she could ruin lives with her reality. Some nights before putting Aria to bed, Chandra would tell her made-up stories of how their lives should be with a mother and father and family trips to Disney World. She would tell Aria all about this made-up world she lived in because her reality was too hard swallow.

A few years have passed. Clarissa was pregnant. She and Ray were in a better place, and Chandra was safe again. Clarissa had to stop working due to her difficult pregnancy, and Ray had gotten two jobs. He was never around, and Chandra and Aria got to spend all their free time with their mom. This allowed Granny Ann and Grandpa John to spend most of their time out of state and their vacation home. Uncle Joseph was now off living his own life. He was never around or in the same state anymore. Aria's pain and medication was being monitored and maintained by her at home nurse's aide. Things were looking up. This had been the absolute best seven months of Chandra's life. Clarissa had to stop working after she found out she was two months pregnant. She was now at the end of her pregnancy and about to have her baby.

One day while watching television, Clarissa felt as if she was going to be sick, so she was rushed to the hospital with belly pains. The doctor told her the terrible news that she had lost the baby that was inside of her. She was still made to deliver her beautiful baby. Ray and Clarissa were devastated. They had a small funeral service for their baby and buried her in the family cemetery. Six months later, Clarissa went back to work. She mourned the loss of her baby girl, but she knew that she had to pick herself up for the other two girls that needed her now. Ray ended up going back to having one job. The second job that he had acquired laid him off. They picked up their lives and went back to living again. Chandra wondered what this would mean for her. She had become accustomed to coming home to her mom being there and feeling safe. Now, her life would become chaotic and sad again. It didn't take long for Ray to start up with Chandra again. Things were just as bad as before, and there was no light at the end of Chandra's tunnel.

Chandra was now fourteen years old. Her life was filled with pain and sadness. She walked around with this secret that only she could know. One day while walking home from school, Chandra noticed a police car sitting on the side of the road. She never really paid attention, but for some reason, this car and this policeman caught her attention. He was watching her. She was sure that she had done nothing wrong, but for some reason, he brought fear inside of her. To get home, Chandra had to walk down this path. She was told to take that way because it kept her from walking on the busy road with cars that would be speeding by. Chandra kept walking by the policeman as if she didn't see him sitting in his car. He shouted out, "Come here, little girl."

Chandra knew it was a cop, so she'd better listen to him. He placed Chandra in the back of his squad car and drove her down the path and made her pull her clothes off and raped her. He smelled of old spice and peppermint. His hands were rough like sandpaper. He told her he simply wanted to see how it felt to be with a black girl. She felt that maybe this was her punishment, and the God that she heard about on Sunday mornings had forgotten all about her. Maybe he hated her for allowing these men to continue to do these things to her. She was utterly destroyed. I would like to say this was the last time this cop did this, but this continued on for some months. Chandra figured he must have been assigned to some other unit because he stopped coming around her side of town. It was a relief, but she was so used to being taken advantage of, she didn't even care anymore.

This time in her life, she was simply a shell of a person. She would walk around with the biggest smile on her face and being the biggest encourager to those around her. She knew that she had to be strong for those that she loved. She was always told that if she let anyone in on what was going on, she could destroy her family. Chandra was exhausted inside. She spent her entire life protecting everyone and keeping secrets. She knew that she didn't want anyone in the world to be in as much pain as she was, so she stayed quiet. Chandra had a way about her, the old folks called it an old soul. She would light up any room simply by walking in. When someone was having a bad day, they knew they could call on Chandra. Granny Ann would talk with Chandra in the afternoon and ask all types of questions, but as much as she loved Chandra, she just couldn't put her finger on what was wrong.

Clarissa was still mourning the loss of her baby girl and wanted to adopt a baby. She talked it over with Ray, he felt that the idea was a great one. They immediately found someone willing to allow them to adopt their baby. She was already pregnant and just so happened to be looking for a family for her baby girl. As the months passed, the young lady, Clarissa, and Ray filled out all the necessary paperwork, completed all the home studies, and even attended some classes that would council them on what it all meant. And how to overcome any obstacles they may encounter. The day had finally come, and it was time to pick up their baby girl from the hospital. The mom was currently in labor, and Clarissa, Ray, Aria, and Chandra were all in the waiting room of the hospital. It felt like forever because Chandra and Aria were asking a million questions. The nurse came from the back area and told Ray and Clarissa their baby was finally here. She had arrived in eight pounds six ounces. She was a healthy one. They had to wait for the baby to be washed and checked out before they could go to the back and see her.

When they were finally allowed back in the room, Aria and Chandra had to remain in the waiting area. It would be three days before the girls got to meet their baby sister. They had decided to name her Aryanna. The night before Aryanna was to arrive home, Clarissa decided to spend the night with the baby at the hospital with the biological mother. She wanted to be in the room all night with them. The hospital gave her a pillow and a blanket. Chandra and Aria were to stay home with Ray. Chandra already knew the routine and what was going to happen. She took her shower and awaited her fate. That night, after all was said and done, Chandra began planning her escape.

The next morning, Clarissa arrived with their new baby sister. There was so much joy. Aria was so happy. She had someone to boss around now. She knew the love Chandra had for her because she now had that same love for Aryanna. Granny Ann was back in town as well. Grandpa John was over the moon. Grandpa Dan even stopped by to see his newest granddaughter. Chandra loved to see the joy plastered on everyone's faces. She knew that new life had brought new joy. She had a huge smile on her face, partly because of the joy going around the room. And also the joy she had knowing that her pain would soon be over.

She had decided that it all had to end. She knew what she wanted to do, and how she wanted to do it. She knew that she couldn't take it anymore. Granny Ann, as usual, noticed the happiness that Chandra was now exhibiting and was watching her with a perplexed look on her face. Chandra reassured her that all was well, and she was just happy about her new sister. Granny Ann, desperately wanting this to be true, decided to let well enough alone. Days and weeks, and months rolled by. Chandra's birthday was quickly approaching, and she would be turning fifteen years old. She had begun riding to school with her cousins so that she wouldn't have to walk anymore. She was so happy about that. Although her cop had stopped coming around, she didn't want a repeat with any other cop. She was planning to have a bunch of friends, girls and boys, over for her birthday. She was an athlete, so she had made many friends during cheer as well as track. She wanted them all at her birthday party.

The day had arrived, and Chandra was over the moon. Clarissa had gone all out and cooked so many amazing dishes. She also had all of Chandra's friends over to celebrate with her. Chandra knew the night couldn't last long because Mom had to go to work, and everyone had school the next morning. Granny Ann had Aryanna and Aria for the night. Aria was supposed to attend Chandra's party, but she decided at the last minute to help out with the baby. Chandra understood and gave them both big hugs and kisses and told them goodbye.

Aria, as usual, said, "No goodbyes, only catch you later."

That was something she and Chandra did every time she would get admitted into the hospital. The party ended, and it was time for Clarissa to go to work. Chandra watched her mom get dressed for work. She watched her put on makeup and brush her hair and talked to her the entire time. She told her mom that she had planned on having four children when she grow up, two girls and two boys, but now she decided that she didn't want any children. Clarissa laughed at that, thinking she was only saying that because she had to help raise her little sisters. Clarissa went off to work. Ray was asleep in the bedroom. Chandra knew that he usually woke up around 1:00 to 2:00 a.m. to molest her. She wasn't going to wait around for that to happen. Chandra took an entire bottle of Tylenol or what was left of it. She drifted off to sleep. She couldn't keep her eyes open. She was finally free from it all.

There was so much light. Too much light. Chandra couldn't understand what was going on. So many people were talking. Why are they all looking at her? Wait, why is she awake? What is happening? Had she even failed at her attempt to end it all? She overheard the doctor telling her mom and Granny Ann that if it had been just a few more pills, she wouldn't be here. It was also at this moment that Granny Ann and Clarissa found out that Chandra had been pregnant and unfortunately, had lost the baby. Ray, Chandra wants to know where is Ray.

Please, Lord, don't let Ray be alone with Aria and Aryanna.

Clarissa notices Chandra eyes open, and her mouth is moving. "What, baby?" Clarissa asked.

Chandra can't speak. Her throat hurts so bad. They had shoved tubes as well as charcoal down her throat to make her puke. She mouthed the word, *Ray.*

Clarissa said, "Ray found you and is worried sick. He's out in the waiting room with Grandpa and the girls."

Chandra was relieved to know that he was not alone with the girls. Grandpa John and Grandpa Dan would protect them. It took a few days, but Chandra was back home with Clarissa and Grandma Ann. They wanted to know what was going on. They wanted to know what happened. They wanted to know who she was pregnant by. Who was the baby's father. They just wanted some answers on why they almost lost their little girl. Her entire life, as far as she could remember, Chandra had been keeping a journal filled with stories and poems about everything that had happened to her. She handed this to her Granny Ann. She told Granny Ann that all the answers were in those journals. During this time, Aria walked in and said, "It was never a dream, was it Chandra?"

A little confused, Chandra asked, "What do you mean, Aria?"

Aria now raises her voice with tears in her eyes, "It was *never* a dream, was it?"

Chandra was now taken back to that night years ago when Aria walked in.

Chandra drops her head and said, "Yes."

Aria raced over and grabbed Chandra and hugged her, and they both just cried. Clarissa and Granny Ann were crying too, watching their girls so broken. Aria then began to tell Clarissa and Granny Ann what she saw. Clarissa was fuming and wanted details about it all. Chandra began from the beginning. They were all in the room for hours. Eventually, Grandpa John came in to find out what was going on and to alert the women to baby Aryanna being awake. He was startled to find the women in his life crying and looking as if they had seen a ghost. He immediately asked what was going on. Granny Ann distracted him, as only she can, and told him she will discuss the matter later.

Clarissa was a mess. She walked in the room to grab Aryanna with Granny Ann and collapses on the floor in a flood of tears.

Granny Ann grabbed the baby out of the crib and allowed Clarissa to cry and gather herself. She left Clarissa in the room to herself while she tended to the baby. During this time, Chandra and Aria were in the other room, scared. They don't know what was going to happen now that Granny Ann and Clarissa knew their secret. Aria was talking Chandra about why she never told her the truth, and Chandra was trying to explain to Aria what was going on in her head at the time. Chandra would have never told any of this information. She wanted to end her life in hopes that everyone would be able to live on and be happy. In her mind, she was the problem. She was the reason for all this happening. In these moments, Chandra wished she had succeeded at her suicide attempt. She knew that this would be a disaster and a lot of pain.

As the day went on, Clarissa and Granny Ann discussed how to go forward with the situation. Clarissa knew that if the men in her life knew what happened, they would end up behind bars. She couldn't be the cause of that. She decided that she would come up with a lie to tell everyone, and they would move on with their lives. She called a family meeting that night. Ray had no idea that he was outed and that he was going to be put out of the house. He just knew that Clarissa had something to discuss with the entire family. That night, the family, Granny Ann, Grandpa John, Clarissa, Chandra, Aria, Aryanna, and Ray gathered at Granny Ann's house to have this family meeting. Clarissa gathered everyone in the living room. She had everyone sit down, and Granny Ann had all the girls around her. Ray was off in the corner by himself.

Clarissa began to speak, "Ray and I have decided that we will be separating."

Ray was shocked and immediately jumped up and said, "Separating, who decided that?"

Clarissa said, "Due to information that was told to me today by Chandra, I think Ray would want to separate."

Ray's eyes were widened, and he sat down. He knew or had a feeling that Chandra had told on him finally. Grandpa John looked confused as well but decided not to say anything. He knew that something happened but wanted to wait to talk with Granny Ann about it. Clarissa left the girls to Granny Ann's for the night while she and Ray went home to talk.

When Clarissa and Ray arrived at home, Ray immediately started to lying.

"Baby, I don't know what that girl has told you, but you know that she lies. She is mad at me because I punished her for talking to boys."

Clarissa was looking at Ray with disgust and simply ask him to pack his bags. She told him that she was doing him a favor by not alerting the authorities and putting his behind in jail. Although Clarissa was upset, she still wasn't all the way certain that she believed Chandra. Her heart wanted to believe her, but her heart also loved and believed Ray. Ray packed his bag and sat on the end of the bed in their bedroom. Clarissa was sitting in the bed under the covers. Ray began to talk to Clarissa about their love and how he never touched Chandra. He told her that it was all a lie and a misunderstanding. He spent hours crying and begging Clarissa and telling lie after lie. He knew that he was making some progress because Clarissa had not asked him to leave her alone yet. So he continued to try and break down those walls to her heart.

Eventually, Clarissa told Ray that she was tired and needed him to leave because she had a lot to think about. He knew that he had touch her heart in some way because she was no longer furious with him. He got his bag, that only had about three days of clothes in it, and he left. Ray gave Clarissa a few days to cool off. He didn't contact her or stopped by the house. During this time, they told the family that Ray spanked Chandra and that's why Clarissa made him leave. It seemed like the better option to tell the family the lie instead of the truth. Chandra had been staying with Granny Ann and Grandpa John. She was still not comfortable with going home. The entire week went by and things seemed to be going to normal or as normal as possible. Clarissa went back to work, Chandra went back to school, and Aria and Aryanna continued to go to Granny Ann's during the day to be babysat. Ray only called Clarissa now to check on Aryanna and doesn't attempt to come over. This went on for a few weeks. Clarissa seemed to be slowly forgiving Ray and believed the lies that he was telling her.

One Saturday night, Clarissa came over to Granny Ann's to discuss things with Chandra. She told Chandra that Ray had apologized for spanking her, and she told Chandra to tell Aria that the night she thought she was asleep, the man just fell on Chandra and that nothing happened. She also convinced Chandra to tell Granny Ann that it was all made up, and she was mad about Ray spanking her for talking to a boy. Chandra loved her mom and didn't want her to be upset, so she did just that. Although Granny Ann didn't believe a word, Chandra was saying to her, she said that she would let it all go. She did, however, let Clarissa know that Chandra would not be moving back in with her.

Ray eventually moved back into the house with Clarissa and moved on with their lives as if nothing happened. He wasn't allowed to be with any of the girls on his own. This was a condition that Clarissa had placed on him upon his return. He was not allowed to babysit or watch any of the girls. If Clarissa left the room and the girls were in there playing, Ray was not allowed to go in and talk to them at any moment unless another adult was present. Granny Ann also made it very clear that Ray was never allowed over her house under any circumstances. Ray agreed to all the terms before being allowed to step foot inside Clarissa's home.

Inside, Chandra was torn. She knew that her mother loved her, but she felt also that her mother had betrayed her by allowing such a man to be a part of her life after what he had done to her. It was evident that Clarissa never took the time to read any of Chandra's writings but Granny Ann sure did. She knew the extent of the abuse, but back in those days you didn't air your dirty laundry to the public, so this matter would remain between them. Granny Ann knew that she had to protect Chandra and that is all she wanted to do. Chandra was growing up and helping Granny Ann as much as she could. Being allowed to stay with Granny Ann was blessing, and Chandra took full advantage of the happiness in her life now. Clarissa came by every night after work to pick up Aria and Aryanna, but she and Chandra never spoke much. An occasional hi and bye. Chandra was getting used to things being that way. She wanted to be bothered by it, but a part of her was relieved. She knew that if she and her mother would talk, many questions would need to be answered.

Chandra was now sixteen years old. Her sweet sixteen was bittersweet. She wanted so much to have the fairy tale party with her mother by her side. Granny Ann made her party as nice as she could, but Clarissa went to work and never had the time to stop by. Clarissa was now working two jobs to support Aria, Aryanna, and Ray. He had lost his job when a coworker accused him of sexual harassment. She said that he tried to rape her when he was giving her a ride to work. He was now living off Clarissa and staying home, drinking most of the time. Chandra tried her best to ignore the fact that her mother was not there and enjoyed herself, but her heart was a little broken. Chandra's aunt, Doreen, was a manager at Walmart, and she attended Chandra's party that night. She told Chandra to come down to the store and get a job the following day. In her small town of Raymond, Georgia, you could work at the age of sixteen. Chandra was excited that she would be working soon.

The very next day, Chandra went down to her local Walmart and applied for the job, did the interview, and got the job all in the same day. She was told to return the next day to do her training and receive her uniform. The uniform consisted of a shirt, a smock, and a name tag. Chandra was on time the following day and ready to work. She was trained by a woman named Kate. Kate was a confident, tall, and loud woman. She was very friendly and took to Chandra right away. Chandra and Kate became great friends despite the twenty-year age difference. Kate took Chandra under her wing.

Kate knew that Clarissa, who was now working in a different department of Walmart, was Chandra's mother. She wanted to ensure that Clarissa and Chandra were okay with working together and that Chandra would be comfortable with her mother. Clarissa assured Kate that Chandra was a hard worker and would not goof off and that she was okay with her taking Chandra under her wings. Chandra loved working. She absolutely enjoyed the thrill of getting out of school and going into work. She knew that every week she would be able to contribute something to her Granny Ann and her mom. She wanted to ensure her sisters never wanted for anything. She didn't even mind that Ray was living with her mom anymore. She knew that eventually her mom would get sick and tired of putting up with his mess and move on.

During her time at work, Chandra met a guy named Tommy. Tommy was very handsome. He didn't attend the same school as Chandra, but she knew him through her job. Tommy was a straight-A student who wanted to go to college after high school. Tommy was a senior, and Chandra was only a junior, but they didn't care about that. They ended up spending all of their time together. When Chandra and Tommy were at work, they would have lunch together. Chandra worked mostly every weekend, but when she would get off work, she and Tommy were connected at the hip. They really enjoyed their time and talks with each other. Tommy's family adored Chandra and always wanted her around. She would even hang out with his mom when Tommy was at work. They had a wonderful relationship. Chandra knew that Tommy would be leaving soon, and this joy was probably short-lived. But she didn't focus on that and decided to live in the moment. They dated the entire year of school.

The time came for the prom, and Tommy asked Chandra to go with him. She was overjoyed. She had declined to go to her own prom because she knew that she still had next year. Tommy and Chandra went shopping one Saturday to pick out their prom clothes together and ran into some of Ray's family. They hated Chandra at this point and blamed her for the demise of Ray. Chandra tried to casually walk past them, but they started calling her whore, slut, and all other names. She was humiliated and walked to the car. Tommy was ready to fight, but Chandra begged him to let it all go and to leave. That night while sitting in his car, Tommy asked Chandra to tell him what all the arguing and name-calling was about. Chandra had never told anyone of her past after discussing it with Clarissa and Granny Ann. She trusted Tommy and told him what had happened to her. He held her in his arms, and for the first time ever, Chandra felt safe inside the arms of another man. She thought that she loved Tommy forever. The night of the prom was here, and Chandra was nervous wreck. Kate, Clarissa, and Granny Ann were all over to help Chandra get dressed. Ari and Aryanna were watching television, unenthused about all that was going on. Clarissa was in charge of Chandra's hair, Kate did her makeup, and Granny Ann gave her the necessary jewelry and shoes to make it all come together. Chandra was breathtaking. She was absolutely gorgeous. Tommy, his mom, Gloria, and his dad, Jim, all came over to take pictures of the couple. They were so happy and excited about these two love birds. As Tommy and Chandra were walking out of the door, Clarissa grabbed Chandra and held her the tightest that she has ever held her and whispered, "I love you more than my own life, and I am sorry more than you'll ever know!"

Chandra said, "I forgive you!"

And she and Tommy went on their way. The night was so much fun. They danced and laughed all night. Chandra felt as if a weight was lifted off her shoulders. She was able to smile. She enjoyed the time she and Tommy were away. Dancing in his arms and pretending her life was one out of a fairy tale. Chandra knew, however, just like everything in life, this too will have to come to an end. The night was long, and Chandra's feet were sore. As Tommy was driving her home, he asked if she wanted to spend the night with him. Chandra had permission to stay out that night from her Granny Ann, but she knew that she wasn't ready for the type of intimacy that Tommy might have wanted. Chandra agreed to spend the night with Tommy if he promised not to try anything with her. He agreed. Tommy and Chandra spent the night at the beach in a beautiful hotel room. As of his word, Tommy respected Chandra and held her all night and talked without the mention of sex.

The next morning came, and the sun was beaming through the window. Tommy and Chandra both had to work the night shift and prepared to get back to their homes and get ready for work. On the drive home, Tommy let Chandra know that he was accepted to a college in Texas and would be leaving in May to live with some family there before moving into college. This broke her heart, but she only wanted the best for Tommy and pretended to be happy for him. When they arrived at Granny Ann's house, Tommy helped Chandra get out of the car and walked her and her bags into the house. He gave her a hug and a kiss and left. A small part of her wished she had slept with him that night knowing he would be leaving in the next month or so. She knew that was just talk in her head because she already missed him. She wasn't ready for that type of relationship.

Chandra and Tommy worked many nights over the next few months which left little time for them to be together. They were both academic achievers and put their grades and studies before anything else in life. They were also both athletes, and for some odd reason, these things were suddenly an overload. When they were together, they were ignoring each other, doing homework, or studying for test. Just to be in each other's presence had to be enough for them. It was finally graduation day, and Tommy was the most handsome guy at the school in his cap and gown. He was the class president and the star of the football team. He was asked to give a speech on graduation day, and he was nervous. Chandra was there to cheer him on, and he was grateful for that. When he walked up to the podium, he glanced the crowd to make sure his eyes were on the love of his life. His speech was all about overcoming struggles and pushing forward. He told of a little girl who, despite her past, had become the most beautiful woman he knew. Chandra thought the story was about her. She smiled and looked over to Tommy's mom whose eyes were filled with tears, and then noticed Tommy's dad holding her hands and realized the story was about her.

Chandra smiled and put her arms around Tommy's mom knowing now that their connection was more than just Tommy. His mom had endured things that Chandra had yet to overcome. She held on to Tommy's mom the entire ceremony. His mom gently rubbed her hand as if she knew Chandra's story. After the ceremony, Tommy's parents decided to have an intimate dinner with a few of Tommy's friends at their home. It was with his four friends, his parents, Chandra, and Clarissa. They had an amazing meal and joked and enjoyed each other. The night was coming to a close, and Clarissa asked Chandra if she wanted to go with her to her house for the night, or would she be spending the night with Tommy and his family. Chandra went to talk it over with Tommy, and he asked her if she would be upset if he chose to go out with his friends. Chandra said no, and she went home with Clarissa. Chandra was nervous because it had been so long since she'd spent the night with her mom. Clarissa assured her that Ray wouldn't be at the house that night.

When they arrived at Clarissa's house, Granny Ann was there. She had decided to come over, and they were all going to have a girl's night. This was a wonderful surprise for Chandra. She got to spend the remainder of the night eating ice cream, cookie dough, candy, and watching movies with the ladies. They ended up watching a bunch of old movies picked out by Granny Ann. They didn't mind. They were spending some much-needed quality time together.

The next morning came, and it was time for Granny Ann to go home, and Chandra had to work. She knew that Tommy would be there to take her to work around 10:00 a.m. because they both had to work the same shift that day. She patiently waited on the front porch for his arrival. As expected, Tommy arrive around 9:30 a. m., ready to roll. She climbed into his Mustang and turned the music down. Chandra and Tommy talked all the way to work which was about a fifteen-minute drive. Tommy told Chandra the news of his departure. They only had two weeks remaining together. He had already given his notice at Walmart and was going to stay until he worked his final shift. Chandra told him that she was sad to see him go but happy to see his dreams come true. They finally arrived at work and kissed each other and were off. The next two weeks were a blur. It seemed to go by way too fast. Chandra was at Tommy's house and saying goodbye. She knew this was going to be hard, but she didn't count on this many tears and for her heart to break as bad as it was. She didn't want to let him go. Tommy's mom and dad were already sitting in the car waiting on Tommy to say his final goodbyes to Chandra and his friends. Tommy's friend, Kory, pulled Chandra back and held her in his arms as the car pulled away and out of the driveway. Chandra, Kory, Kia, and Paul all decided to go and have a meal together at the nearby Zaxby's.

Chandra felt alone even in the midst of all Tommy's friends. They spent the afternoon comforting her and telling her things would be okay. Tommy and his parents eventually arrived in Texas, and he immediately calls Chandra. They spent a few minutes on the phone and then he tells Chandra he was going to bed. It takes two days before Chandra hears from Tommy again. He would text her good morning and good night, but he hasn't been calling or texting really. She figured he was spending time with the family and didn't want to be that girl who was bugging him. He finally called, and they had a very long conversation about his ride there, her lunch with his friends, his family, and all the new members he met. He seemed to be very happy with Texas. They also talked about how much they absolutely missed each other. Chandra told Tommy the news of her moving back in with Clarissa. He was shocked considering he knew all the details of Ray and asked her to please be careful. Chandra, Granny Ann, and Clarissa had discussed Chandra moving back into her mom's home. Ray worked nights at a factory and sleeps all day. Chandra will be able to watch the girls at night if Clarissa had to go to work, and Granny Ann could take a trip with Grandpa John. It was a winning situation for them all at the time. Ray knew the rules and abided by them. He never even spoke to Chandra while she was there.

One day, Ray didn't have to work the night shift and Clarissa did. Chandra thought to herself this might be a problem. She didn't want to sound overly cautious, but she also didn't want to let her guard down and allow something to happen. Chandra told Clarissa it was okay and that she would be able to watch the girls, and she would be okay with Ray in the house. She was older now and knew how to protect herself. While Clarissa was at work, Chandra made sure the girls were bathed and fed and also helped Aria with her homework. Ray never left his bedroom. He didn't even come out to grab a plate of food. As Chandra was helping Aria with the last of her language arts assignment, she got a text on her phone. She looked down and noticed that it was Tommy asking her to call him as soon as she has a free moment. It had been a while now since Tommy had been in college, and for a few weeks, he's been kind of distant. Chandra knew that he was most likely overwhelmed with this new lifestyle and wanted him to be comfortable and confident, so she didn't bother him much. He came home for the holidays and they only spent three days together. Chandra didn't make a big fuss about that either. Tommy said that he loved her, and she trusted him and wanted to make this work. Chandra had to start working mostly weekends only, so she knew the stresses of school. Chandra made sure the girls were in bed and asleep and she made her way to the living room to call Tommy. He answered on the first ring.

"Hey, Chan, what you are doing?"

"Nothing at all. I just got the girls to sleep, and I guess I should finish my homework. What's wrong? Why do you sound so down?"

"I have something to tell you, and I don't know how to let you know."

"Whatever it is, we will deal with it together. What's wrong, baby?"

"Here goes, I went to a party that was for Thanksgiving, and I wanted to let go and have fun. We had won the game that night, and we were celebrating our success."

"Yes, Tommy. I remember that."

"I ended up getting wasted. I don't drink, but I was taking shots with some of my teammates. I don't even remember it happening, but I know it did."

"What happened Tommy?"

By this time, Chandra is choked up and bracing herself for the news she had already suspected but wouldn't let her mind accept.

"I spent the night with this girl, and now she's pregnant."

Chandra just sat in silence. She didn't say a word. Everything went silent. She didn't even hear as Tommy was calling her name. She hanged up the phone. She couldn't talk to him right now. She had to keep her mind focused. She knew that Ray was in the house, and she had to protect her sisters. She gathered herself. She's used to this. This was hurt. This feeling was familiar. She had given into happiness, in her mind, and in her heart, she knew that feeling couldn't last. This was real, this was her life. For a brief moment in her life, she almost thought she could be happy. She had begun to accept that happiness. What a fool. What an idiot. No, Chandra knew she couldn't allow anything to bring her out of protection mode on this night. Chandra turned the ringer off of the house phone and slowly made her way into the girls' room and placed a blanket on the floor and drifted off to sleep. She was awakened by the knocking on the room door.

It was morning, and Clarissa was home. She was waking them all up to get ready for school. Chandra was grateful because she had forgotten to set her alarm. As Chandra was getting dressed for school, she pretended the last night didn't happen. She forgot that she had turned the ringer off of the phone at the house.

She thought to herself, *Oh well, I'm sure mom won't answer it, anyways.*

She knew that while the nurses and teachers were taking care of Aria, Mom usually allowed the television to watch Aryanna. Ray was home today, and as long as he was in the presence of Mom, he was allowed to help with the girls. Chandra went through her day and her classes with a smile on her face. Everyone always thought she was the happiest girl in the world. It was easy to smile and pretend her world wasn't falling apart. She was heartbroken, but this familiar feeling wasn't going to stop her.

When Chandra returned home from school, Clarissa was awake and Ray was gone for the night. This was almost a relief because Chandra was exhausted and had no fight or protector inside of her. She only wanted to take a shower and go to bed. She didn't want to feel. She came in and played with Aryanna and talked with Aria. She wanted to tell her mom about Tommy but didn't want her mom to see him in a negative way. She was still unsure of how she was going to handle that entire situation. She didn't even know if Tommy still wanted to be with her. He has a baby on the way. What if he wants to marry this new girl? Does he still talk to this new girl? What is the status of their relationship? She had so many questions going around and around in her head. Chandra decided to take a shower and go to bed. After she had fallen asleep for a few hours, she heard a knock at her bedroom door. She got up and opened the door to find Clarissa standing there with the cordless phone in her hand.

"No, Mom, I don't want to talk to anyone."

Clarissa said, "It's Tommy, sweetie."

Not wanting to explain things to Clarissa yet, Chandra grabbed the phone and said thank you. She closed the door to her bedroom and immediately hangs up the phone. She knew that if the other phone rings, Clarissa will run to pick it up. She waited for the ring. She waited and waited, but it didn't ring. Whew, that was a relief.

A few days went by and Chandra didn't hear from Tommy. She figured he's moved on with his new girl and they were going to have a great life together. Chandra was upset but wasn't ready to talk to anyone about her feelings yet. She decided to drown herself in her sisters and her schoolwork. It was close to Chandra's birthday, and she was not looking forward to doing anything. She didn't even realize that the day was so close. In two days, she will be seventeen years old. Fun times weren't even in her mind. All she could think of these days was staying busy. She knew that if she took the time to think about anything she would break.

The day of Chandra's birthday had finally arrived. She had decided to have a nice dinner with her mom and sisters. She had hoped Granny Ann and Grandpa John would have returned by now. Grandpa Dan hadn't been feeling well and had been ordered to rest for a while. Chandra decided to cook her meal herself. She knew that Clarissa had worked the night before and wanted to give her a break. It meant enough to Chandra that Clarissa had sent Ray to spend the weekend looking after his ill mother. She knew that with him away Chandra would be able to enjoy her birthday much more. Chandra spent the day in the kitchen making her best soul food meals. Cooking was her passion. She loved to smell the food as it was cooking and then watching the faces of everyone around her enjoying her hard work. She was absolutely in her element today.

The food was coming along very well. Dinner was to be around 5:00 p.m., and things were looking like they were going to be done right on time. Chandra had prepared a feast. She made fried chicken, mac 'n' cheese, collard greens, barbecue ribs, mashed potatoes, corn bread, red velvet cake, chocolate cake, and some southern sweet tea. As Chandra was preparing the table, she heard the doorbell ring. Who could it be? The girls were home, and Clarissa was asleep. Chandra's best friend was away visiting family, and her other friends were at Disney World for a band competition. Chandra made her way to the front door, and when she opened the door, she was in shock. It was everyone she could think of. Her best friend, Jessica, some of her teammates, her Granny Ann, Grandpa John, Grandpa Dan, and Tommy and his parents. She was both excited and annoyed. Clarissa didn't know what happened between her and Tommy, so Chandra was sure that Clarissa had invited them all. Chandra decided to let the party go on with a smile. She was overjoyed to see everyone else. Chandra set the table. She was glad that she took the time to prepare so much food. As everyone began eating, Chandra slipped away and took a shower and changed her clothing. She was filthy from the flour and cooking oils and cooking. When she had returned, everyone was in full conversations. They were all having an amazing time. Tommy and his family were deep into conversations with Granny Ann and Grandpa John about their recent vacation adventures. Chandra decided to join Jessica at the table.

The two of them had gotten so caught up in school and track until they hadn't really talked about serious issues lately. They began talking about the colleges they were accepted to and where they planned to attend for their futures. Eventually, the teammates made their way into the conversation, and it was all about colleges and futures. Two of Chandra's teammates were considering attending the University of Texas with Tommy. Chandra played it off with a smile as if she was excited about that. She hadn't spoken to Tommy, and at this point, was unsure of what she wanted to do as far as the relationship. The night went on, and everyone was having a great time, but all good things must end. Everyone started to leave and were giving their hugs and goodbyes. Chandra noticed that Tommy wasn't leaving but his parents were.

She thought to herself, *Who's taking him home?*

As soon as the last guest had walked out the door, Clarissa gave Chandra the biggest hug and said, "Good night sweetie. The girls and I are going to bed. I made up the pull-out couch for Tommy."

Chandra was nervous, angry, and excited all at once. She started cleaning up the kitchen as if she didn't see Tommy standing there. He began helping her. He didn't know where to begin. Tommy asked Chandra if it was okay to give her a hand with the dishes. She accepted the help, and they cleaned the entire kitchen in silence. There was the occasional "excuse me" or "sorry" spoken but nothing of importance. The kitchen was now clean, and Chandra was wiping down the counters. Tommy walked up behind her and grabbed her waist. This feeling of security was all too familiar to her. She wanted to cry and scream at him, but she needed this. She needed to know that he wanted and missed her as much as she wanted and missed him. They stood there for what seemed like forever. His arms around her waist, his face buried in her hair and neck, and tears falling down both their faces. No words were spoken. Eventually, they knew someone had to move, and someone had to speak. Chandra walked out of Tommy's embrace and turned to look at him. She wanted to say so much, but all that came out was, "You know where the towels are. You can take your shower, and we can talk later."

Chandra walked to her room to put her jammies on. She had a feeling this would be a long night.

Chandra walked into to living room. Tommy was sitting on the fold-out bed with the remote in his hand, but he hadn't turned the television on. Chandra sat on the bed in front of him. At first, he just hung his head. He looked up and began telling Chandra what happened the night of the game. He went into all the details of him drinking, passing out, and waking up beside a stranger. He vaguely remembered talking to the girl at the party, but they woke disoriented and unclothed. He knew they had made the mistake of sleeping together but couldn't recall the details of the night. The girl, whose name was Autumn, couldn't remember anything either. Tommy went on for what seemed like forever. Chandra sat looking him in the eyes the entire time. She hadn't noticed the tears that were streaming down her face. When Tommy stopped talking, she noticed the bed beneath her was soaking wet with the pain she allowed to flow from her eyes.

Chandra asked, "What now?"

Tommy explained that he wanted nothing to do with Autumn, but he was going to take care of their baby. Tommy's parents had agreed to watch the baby so that Tommy could finish school. Autumn had decided to sign over all her parental rights to this child once he was born. After this semester, Tommy would transfer to the local university so that he could help his parents with the baby. The baby was due in a few months. Chandra was going to be graduating and moving away in a few months. Tommy desperately wanted Chandra to choose a college closer to him in Georgia. Chandra and Tommy talked all night and came to the conclusion that neither of them were willing to give up on their relationship due to one mistake. They hugged, and Chandra went to her room to go to bed.

The next morning came, and Chandra took Tommy home. They decided to start over. She had to learn to trust him again. She knew this was going to be hard, but she was willing to try considering he was the first guy that she'd ever loved, and she thought this was the real thing. She knew that he would be leaving for Texas in a few hours, but she didn't want to think about that now. Before she could pull out of his driveway, he asked her to open her birthday present from him. She didn't want to, but she gave in and did it, anyways. It was a charm bracelet that read, "Forgiven, and forever loved!"

Chandra smiled and asked, "What if I hadn't forgiven you?"

They both just laughed, and he pulled her in for a kiss and held her for what seemed like forever. Chandra knew that she was still broken, but she wanted this, and she wanted him.

Graduation day came. All graduates were gathering inside the cafeteria preparing for their final walk. They were all looking out at the football stadium at the crowds of people gathering in the stands. Chandra was excited. Tommy and his parents should be arriving soon. They were scheduled to leave Texas with all his belongings yesterday. They probably made it in extremely late. Chandra hadn't been able to get ahold of any of them. Hopefully, they'll arrive before Chandra began to sing her song. She was a nervous wreck. Why did she let them talk her into singing for the graduation? The band began to play, and the graduates were walking out on the field. Chandra was in the middle, and as she was looking around, she spotted her family. Everyone made it. She was so excited. Kate, her supervisor, and friend were the loudest one in the crowds. As Chandra was looking in the stands and with her family and friends, she didn't see Tommy or his parents. She was getting worried but had to focus on the song. When they called her name, Chandra made her way to the podium and began to sing. She did an amazing job and took her seat. She was so happy that it was over. The graduation went over really quick. The graduates were released, and Chandra raced to her family to see if any of them had heard from Tommy or his family. No one had.

The graduation dinner was going to held at Clarissa's house that day. Everyone was to go home and change into comfortable clothing and come over to enjoy a barbecue at the house. When Chandra arrived home to change her clothes, she noticed a message on her answering machine. She immediately listened to it. Autumn went into labor as Tommy and his family were leaving, and they had to turn around. Her baby boy was born around 9:00 a.m., and he was seven pounds two ounces. Tommy said it was the most amazing thing he had ever witnessed, and he would call Chandra back soon. He congratulated her on graduation and said he knew she would sing amazingly. That was the end of the message. Chandra thought to herself, she would have loved for him to be there, but she understood why he wasn't.

Chandra enjoyed the barbecue with family and friends, but the biggest part of her was away with Tommy. She wanted so bad for him to be there with her celebrating. She felt a ting of selfishness know-ing that she wanted him there and not with the baby or Autumn. Chandra had to shake that off. That was not the way to think about things. After the barbecue was over, Chandra helped Clarissa clean up the mess the guests had left. She cleaned up fast in hopes that later on she would receive a call from Tommy. It was getting close to 8:00 p.m., and the phone hadn't rung yet. Chandra was trying to be patient and not call Tommy's aunt house. It was 8:23 p.m., and the phone started to ring. Chandra ran as fast as she could to answer it. It was indeed Tommy. He told her all about the baby's birth but sounded a little distracted.

Chandra asked, "What's wrong?"

And Tommy told her that Autumn now wanted to keep her baby, and be a part of the baby's life. Chandra wanted to be support-ive and tried to tell Tommy it will all work out. He also informed her of Autumn's move to Georgia. They all had collectively decided that Autumn, the baby, Autumn's parents, and Tommy would all move to Georgia. Autumn and her parents would live in the guest house of Tommy's parents until they found a place of their own. Again, Chandra tried to keep it positive. She and Tommy talked almost all night. They laughed and had a great conversation. Tommy knew that Chandra had chosen to move to Iowa for school. The university there seemed like a perfect fit for her medical education. It was different, and she wanted to experience something new.

Tommy and his parents were now home with the baby boy named Ky. They seemed so happy. Ky had truly changed their lives. Ky was now two months old and doing very well. Chandra was getting ready to leave for Iowa. She was super excited and sad to be leaving Tommy. They had enjoyed their summer together, in spite of the new challenges. Autumn didn't like Chandra, or the relationship Chandra had with Tommy and his parents. She had begun to have a crush on Tommy and wanted them to be a true family. She had expressed this to Tommy many times. Her parents had purchased their home, and they were living only two blocks away from where Tommy and his parents were living. Just like Tommy, Autumn had enrolled at Georgia university. They were both going to finish their education with the help of their parents. Tommy promised to visit Chandra every chance he got, and she promised the same. Tommy assured Chandra that he had absolutely no interest in Autumn. She was at a point in her relationship that she had to trust him or let him go. She chose to trust him.

Unlike Tommy, Chandra chose not to take her car to her first year of college. Most colleges wouldn't allow it, anyways. To her surprise, Iowa University would. She was scheduled that day to board the plane around noon. This was it. She was actually leaving this place. Tommy was the only one to go to the airport with Chandra. She couldn't take her family being there. She knew that she would not be able to stop crying. She would no longer be able to protect her sisters, but Granny Ann had promised to be her eyes and ears. Clarissa had recently switched to day shift, so she knew the girls would be in good hands. The last call for boarding had been placed over the loudspeaker, and Chandra and Tommy said their final good-byes. Chandra was a nervous wreck.

Over the next year, Chandra had grown fond of Iowa. Tommy kept to his word, and every break that he got, he was in Iowa with Chandra. She came home for Christmas and Aria's birthday, but she stayed away as much as possible. Chandra was loving Iowa. She could see this being her forever home. Tommy was trying his best to keep Autumn's hands off him. She was still pursuing him and using Ky to do it. She would often pretend something was wrong with Ky, just to keep Tommy by her side. They were co-parenting with the help of their parents, but Tommy didn't want anything to do with Autumn, just his baby. Chandra was starting to feel like maybe she was being selfish with Tommy, and maybe she should let him see where the relationship with Autumn would lead. That thought quickly passed when Tommy made a surprise visit to Iowa and proposed to Chandra. She said yes, of course. They both wanted to wait until they graduated to get married, but they were ecstatic; the commitment of marriage had been made. Both Chandra and Tommy's parents said they knew that this would happen one day. The two of them knew it would not come without challenges.

Over the next three years of Chandra's college, she and Tommy planned their big day. They were getting the flowers, the pastor, the vows, and everything else that belongs in a wedding. Chandra was to walk across the stage in June and return to Georgia. They wanted a winter wedding, so December would be the time to get married. Chandra knew that Autumn would be a problem. She had already pulled every trick in the book to break them up. She sent Chandra photos of Tommy in bed asleep, as if she was in the room with him. She faked a pregnancy, knowing they hadn't even slept together. She told everyone that Tommy proposed to her, and all her lies were rebutted.

Chandra returned home in June, ready to get back to those she loved. She was so happy to be back with Tommy and her sisters. Granny Ann picked her up from the airport. She couldn't have been happier. When Granny Ann saw her, she grabbed her and immediately began crying. Chandra couldn't understand what was going on. This was supposed to be the best day of her life. She was home. She was back with her loved ones. She was a college graduate and had already secured a job at the hospital around the corner from their house. It was a great day. Granny Ann told Chandra, "Let's get the bags and talk in the car."

Chandra was scared. As they sat in the parking garage, Granny Ann began to speak.

She said, "Baby girl, I'm sorry."

She couldn't finish her story. She broke down again. Chandra was getting impatient and just wanted to know what was wrong. Granny Ann had to tell her what happened. Tommy and his parents were watching Ky for the weekend and preparing to throw a huge dinner party for Chandra's return. Autumn and her parents were also invited because they had become a part of the family because of Ky. Everyone seemed fine, even Autumn was helping out as much as possible. They were all aware of Autumn's obsession with Tommy but ignored it because it wasn't reciprocated. The family were all going and coming from the stores all day. Clarissa and the girls even stopped by and helped a little. Granny Ann said that she and Grandpa John dropped off some food items, and everything seemed fine. Late Saturday night, Autumn asked if they could all have dinner on Sunday before Chandra came home, and everyone agreed.

Granny Ann, Grandpa John, Clarissa, Aria, Aryanna, Tommy's parents, Autumn's parents, Tommy, Ky, and Autumn all had dinner together. Chandra remembered that because Tommy told her he loved her and would see her Monday afternoon. Everyone was starting to show up for dinner. She was sad that she was missing the festivities. That night at dinner, Granny Ann said Autumn was extremely happy. She couldn't put her finger on it. Granny Ann told Chandra that the dinner was nice, and she and Grandpa John and Clarissa and the girls took their leave. They wanted to get some sleep for the next day. Then, Granny Ann got quiet again.

She grabbed Chandra's hand. "Baby girl, they're gone."

Chandra was confused and asked, "Who? Who's gone?"

Her throat catches, and she's about to cry. Granny Ann explained that when they woke up this morning, the news said there was a murder suicide. Autumn had killed Tommy, his parents, her parents, her baby, and then herself. She was unstable. The note she left behind stated they were all to be together for the rest of their lives. Chandra was mess. She was completely beside herself. She couldn't handle this type of pain. She couldn't take this hurt. She began screaming, and she couldn't stop. Granny Ann tried to console her, but there was not helping her right now.

The waves were crashing against the rocks. The sun was shining. The air smelled new. Chandra was in her thoughts. She was sitting on her back deck, enjoying her cup of coffee, and thinking of her life. She was finally at a place in her life where she could smile again. It had been five years since she watched the love of her life be buried. She lost her joy that day. The day after the funeral, Chandra left Georgia. Her heart wouldn't allow her to stay there, knowing her love was gone. She was only twenty-two years old and wanted to get as far away as possible. All her dreams and future plans were buried with Tommy. Chandra now lived in Florida. She's a nurse in the NICU. She loved working with her babies. They took her mind and focus off all her pain. Chandra decided she would never date or fall in love again, and she had kept that promise for five years. Aria was there for the summer to visit Chandra. She came to visit often. Granny Ann had been spending lots of time in Florida as well. Grandpa John died two years prior with cancer. Chandra did make it home in time for the funeral but left immediately after. Clarissa was now divorced and dating some man from their local church. He's an older gentleman, but he treated her very well. Chandra approved of him. They had visited as well. Chandra's home at the beach was usually the family's get away for the summer. This summer will be no different. Aryanna was to arrive in a few days to join her sisters. Clarissa and Steve will join shortly after. Granny Ann had decided to come later so that she could bring Grandpa Dan. He had a few doctors' appointments before they can get on the road.

Everyone had made it to Chandra's house to enjoy a few weeks together for the summer. This was a great time for them all to get caught up and smile. Chandra had taken a few days off to get to know the stranger that Aryanna had brought to the house this summer. Her little sister was just like her mom. She was in love with being in love. It seemed like every other month there was new guy.

Who is the catch of the week this time? His name was Dayle. Dayle was a slender gentleman with light skin and blue-grey eyes. He was quite handsome and very polite. This let Chandra knew that he wouldn't be around long. Aryanna never stayed with the good ones for very long. Clarissa and Steve were too cute together. They really enjoyed each other's company, and he doted over here. She was glowing and seemed very happy with him. Granny Ann and Grandpa Dan seemed to have rekindled their romance as well. They were this beautiful picture of the past. They had both loved and lost. Aria also had a surprise show up to Chandra's house. Her current guy friend Shaun had decided he wanted to take things to another level and showed up with flowers and candy. Aria was elated. The only one without love was Chandra. She wasn't currently looking for love either. The week went on and the family enjoyed their vacation, and everyone left with love in their hearts and joy on their faces. Chandra was always happy to see them come and even happier to see them go.

The workweek went very well for Chandra when she returned after her family's visit. During her final shift on Friday, Chandra ran into a young man named Damien. Damien was very good-looking to the eyes. Damien was not someone Chandra usually noticed as being her type. He was tall, and you could tell that he spent his off time at the gym. Chandra noticed him walking the halls of the hospital. She thought that he may be the family of a patient or a friend of one. She ran into him and knocked all the papers out of her arms. As they bent down to pick them up, his cologne smacked her dead in her face. Chandra looked right into his eyes. She thanked him for helping her and quickly walked away. Chandra was now battling with herself. She had told herself that she would never fall in love again. She didn't even want to date. Her heart was still a block of ice, and she didn't know if anyone could melt it. As Chandra sat in her living room, she was constantly thinking of Damien. The smell wouldn't let her go. She knew that she wasn't mentally ready for a relationship. It would be selfish of her to try and date right now when her heart was still broken.

Chandra wanted to get some advice and who better to talk about love but Clarissa. Chandra knew too well how much Clarissa loved to be in love. It was usually with the wrong person, but she was in love nonetheless. Chandra called Clarissa, and they talked for hours. At the end of the conversation, Clarissa told Chandra that she had to stop punishing herself for what happened to Tommy and his family. Chandra had been holding on to that guilt for way too long. Chandra decided that maybe it was time to give someone a chance to love her again. She wanted to know the feeling once more, of waking up anxious just to look into another person's eyes. Chandra laughed at the thought of falling for a man that she didn't even know who he was. It was a chance encounter, and she may never see this man again. She couldn't have been more wrong.

The next day at work, Chandra walked the same hallway that she had bumped into Damien in, just for the chance to accidentally see him again. If he was a family member of a patient, he would most definitely have to take this way to get to the patient's room. All day long, Chandra took that specific hallway. She walked down on her lunch and when she was going grab more equipment for her babies. It was nearing the close of business, and Chandra was ready to give up on meeting Damien again. She decided to give it one more time and walked down that hallway on her way out of the door. To her surprise, there he was in his scrubs and a stethoscope around his neck, walking down the hall. She was excited and nervous all at once. When did he began working here? She had never seen him before.

As he approached her, he said, "Hi, gorgeous, nice to see you again."

Chandra wanted to melt but kept it cool and simply waved her hands. She wanted to scream and smile and ask him out, but fear kept her from moving. As she walked by, Damien grabbed her hand. She quickly turned around and smiled. He asked her if he would be too bold to get her number. Chandra quickly agreed and handed him a torn piece of paper with her number already written on it. They both giggled at the fact that she had her number prepared in hopes of running into him. Chandra finally spoke up and said, "Make sure you use it soon."

She then walked away. She couldn't believe that she had been that honest with him. She had been reserved for so long. She wanted to get to know him, and she felt she was too old to play games.

Over the next few months, Chandra and Damien kept it strictly to phone conversations. They didn't want to move to fast. Chandra found out that Damien did, in fact, work at the hospital, and he was just signed on as the doctor to the emergency unit. He was on loan for the time being from his hometown of Vermont. He had the option to stay in Florida, and he was trying to make up his mind. Chandra was falling for him hard, and it was just over phone conversations. Chandra and Damien decided to finally get together for their first date. They wanted to keep it open and in public, so they decided to have a date at the Starbucks. Chandra wanted to talk with Damien face-to-face. They were both excited about this coffee date. Chandra was extremely nervous because of how long it had been since she had opened up to anyone.

Today was the day. Chandra was putting on something simple like a pair of jeans and T-shirt. She didn't want to seem to dress up. When she arrived, she noticed that Damien hadn't arrived yet. That gave her extra time to look at herself in the mirror and get her eyeliner on. She had failed to do that when at the house. As she was applying her eyeliner, she looked up, and there was Damien walking into the Starbucks. Clearly, he hadn't seen her sitting in her car. Her nerves were now on one hundred. Damien was so handsome and was dressed casual like Chandra, so she was relieved at her choice in clothing. Chandra proceeded to exit her vehicle and walk inside. To her surprise, Damien had already placed his order.

She must have had a questioning look on her face because he began to explain that he saw what she had ordered on the staff's coffee run, and he already knew what she liked. Chandra thought that was kind of sweet, and it also let her know that he must have liked her as much as she liked him. Damien and Chandra ended up having an amazing conversation and also discovered they had mutual friends. They continued their date for a few hours and finally said good night. Chandra immediately went home and called some of the girlfriends from her job to talk about Damien. She discovered that many of them had heard negative things about him. They told her he was a lady's man and had been dealing with many of the nurses they worked with. Chandra thought to herself that she would not listen to the gossip and would find out for herself. He hadn't shown any of those signs to her in the last month they had been talking. She decided to let go of her fears and move forward.

The weeks continued to flow, and the relationship seemed to progress. Chandra assumed that they were moving at a great rate and thought that the feelings she was having for Damien, he was also having for her. Damien would make trips with his coworkers to the NICU just to see Chandra. And since they shared mutual friends, they often hung out at the same gatherings and dinners together. One night, there was a party being thrown at one of their friend's house, and Chandra and Damien were both attending. Chandra showed up with a few of her girlfriends and said that everyone was outside grilling. Everyone was having an amazing time. Chandra was looking around but couldn't find Damien. She just assumed that he must had to work late and didn't think much else about it. After sitting a while, Chandra noticed Damien's car pull into the driveway, and he stepped out with another girl in the passenger seat.

Chandra was upset but kept her cool and was nice to both of them. Chandra's friends, as well as Damien's friends, couldn't understand what Damien was doing with this girl. They all played it off well. Chandra couldn't stand it after about an hour and decided to leave the party. She went home and fell asleep. Later that night, a few guys from the party, that were mutual friends of hers and Damien, showed up at her door. They came in and tried to talk to Chandra. And told her she deserved better, but she made excuses to them and to herself for Damien. She told them and herself that they never promised to be exclusive, so this was her fault as well as his. She just didn't want to look stupid. The following day, Chandra decided she would act as if nothing happened and moved on from that moment. Apparently, so did Damien. When he called Chandra, he acted as if he wasn't with another woman the night before.

Knowing what everyone was saying about Damien, Chandra already knew that he had slept with this girl. She found out the girl's name was April. Chandra was hurt but tried to keep the smile on her face. Her friends told her to leave him alone, but he sweet-talked his way right back into her heart. Their friends and coworkers knew they were trying to be together and knew that Damien was out there doing his dirt but allowed Chandra to make her own choices. She and Damien would be going in the right direction, and then Damien would find another woman to hurt her with. Chandra continued to take the pain and smile through it.

One night, Chandra decided that she was going to take things to the next level with Damien and went over to his place. She knew that she would be spending the night with him, so she made sure that she packed an overnight bag. As they were watching television, Chandra and Damien heard a knock his door. Damien went to answer the door, and a woman who claimed to be his ex-girlfriend was standing there. She was crying and wanting to talk with Damien. Damien sent her away. She walked around to his bedroom window and began banging on it and begging him to come out and talk to her. Damien asked her to leave a few more times and then asked Chandra to just ignore it. Chandra tried to act as if she wasn't afraid of what the woman could potentially do. She wanted to leave, but every part of her also wanted to stay. She knew she was being stupid for this man but had fallen so hard so fast. She ended up sleeping with Damien that night. A part of her felt like this would keep him from sleeping around, but the biggest and smartest part of her knew this was a mistake. She had given him a part of her that she could never take back.

Damien and Chandra were now a couple, in her mind only. They were still hanging out and spending time with their friends. One night, they all decided to go to the pool hall together to shoot some pool. Damien and Chandra decided to ride in separate cars. He had to work a little late, so she was going to go a little earlier than him. When she showed up, he was already playing pool with some new intern at the hospital. Chandra decided not to pay them any attention and started drinking and talking with their other friends. In true Damien fashion, he left the bar with the intern and went back to her place. Chandra was at this point devastated. She wanted to cry and scream, but how could she? He wasn't truly her man. The next day, she went over to Damien's house to talk to him about what had went down, and he lied about sleeping with this young lady. And this made Chandra feel even worse. She knew then that he could care less about her feelings. After that, Chandra decided to be a little more guarded with her heart. She thought she could play the same game that he was playing and talk to other guys, but she decided in the end that it was not what she wanted to do.

Damien decided to take a trip home for vacation, and Chandra was a little happy to not have to worry about seeing him at the office or out with other girls. He had been putting her on a rollercoaster ride, and her heart was tired of being broken. While Damien was gone to Vermont for vacation, this gave Chandra the chance to get over him. She took every day to get further and further away. She stopped calling and also stopped answering his calls. When he returned, he stopped by her house to have a talk about their relationship. At the end of their conversation, they decided to be exclusive. They decided to give their relationship a real chance. Chandra didn't really understand how they got to that point, but she was willing to try. In her heart, she knew that she would be hurt by him, but a part of her thought she deserved it for her past. Allowing Ray to do what he did to her was deserving of her being hurt for the rest of her life by any man that she allowed in her life.

Chandra and Damien decided that with this new start, they would move in together. They were excited about this new move in their life. They were moving Damien's clothes into Chandra's house one day when one of Chandra's friends called her from the hospital. To let her know that she might want to get tested for a sexually transmitted disease. Chandra was confused about this, and her friend continued to let her know that she had found out that one of the women that Damien had taken to bed had popped hot for Chlamydia. Chandra was livid. She knew that he had been to bed with these women, but now this was putting her life at risk. Stupidly, Chandra talked to Damien about it. He lied about it but agreed to go and get tested, anyways. To both of their surprise, they both tested negative. It wasn't because he didn't sleep with the women, but because he got lucky and didn't contract of pass on the sexually transmitted disease.

With all the women behind them, Damien and Chandra move forward in their relationship. They were now celebrating one year together and decided that it was time to get married. Damien asked Chandra to marry him on her birthday. She was so happy with his proposal. She said yes, she wanted to get married. She didn't want to go through what she went through with Tommy. She decided that she would keep this marriage intimate and quiet. They decided they would get married in front of their friends at the courthouse. Neither of them told their families. They picked a date and went to the courthouse and went and got married. This was an amazing day for them both. They were both so happy. Damien wanted Chandra, and she wanted him. She wanted to believe that he was different and that the love that she showed him would make him love her and only her.

Damien and Chandra decided to visit his family in Vermont and her family in Georgia after six months of marital bliss to give them the good news. Both families were very happy and loved the fact that they had found love. They were so happy that things worked out the way it did. Having their families love them and love their spouse was more than they could have ever asked for. Damien and Chandra knew that both families wanted them to have babies, but they also knew the doctors told them it would be almost impossible for them to conceive. They wouldn't give up hope and would keep trying and praying for a child, but they wouldn't get their hopes up. When they returned from the vacation from their families, Chandra was feeling sick. She didn't understand what was going on, but then she decided to take a pregnancy test. She was indeed pregnant. She and Damien were so happy. They immediately told everyone in their families. Everyone was thrilled. Damien and Chandra's family decided they would all meet in Florida to celebrate the pregnancy of the two.

It was a hot Fourth of July when both families showed up to Damien and Chandra's home. Damien had invited his mom, Regina, his dad, Yasmine, his sister, Stacey, and her two sons, Greg and Joey. Her husband couldn't get the vacation time, so he didn't make this trip. Chandra invited her sister Aria, Aryanna, and their husbands, but they were unable to make it. She also invited Granny Ann, Grandpa Dan, Clarissa, and Steven. Everyone was getting along so well and prepared for a barbecue they would be having later that evening. There was music, laughter, and loads of fun. The children were in the pool, and the families were all sitting around watching them. Chandra had awakened with cramps but decided to just take it easy and not stress for the day. She knew that some women feel cramps when they are stretching, and its usually nothing to worry about. As the families gathered around the table for some good ole barbecue, the children began going in to shower and get dressed in regular clothes. The adults talked and laughed well into the night. After the kids were done eating, they were extremely tired and went to bed.

Chandra stayed awake as long as she could and slowly made her way up to bed herself. It was hot and wet. Why did it feel as if she had peed herself? Chandra jolted awake to find herself drenched in blood. She knew from the amount of blood that she had lost her baby. She knew there was too much blood. She awakened Damien and had him take her to the hospital. When they returned and were walking through the door, Chandra and Damien's moms were both awake and was waiting in the living room. Damien's mom, Regina, immediately stood up and walked over and grabbed Chandra by the arm to guide her to the couch. Clarissa went into the kitchen and grabbed a glass of water for her. Clarissa told Chandra that Granny Ann was upstairs washing the sheets and cleaning the bed. They didn't force Chandra or Damien to talk. They walked off to the kitchen to start breakfast. Damien knew that Chandra wouldn't be able to walk up the stairs to the bedroom, so he walked her into the downstairs' guest room to lay down for a while. When he noticed that Chandra had drifted off to sleep, he went to spend time with the men of the families.

Chandra awakened to see Regina and Clarissa sitting at the end of the bed watching television. She knew they had probably been there the entire day. They all talked for what seemed like forever. They encouraged Chandra and made her feel whole again. She was still heartbroken at the loss of her baby but knew that things would be okay.

The following afternoon, it was time for the families to leave. Heartbroken and weak, Chandra and Damien saw everyone off and tried to pick up the pieces of their heart. The family was a much-needed distraction for them. They decided to try again as soon as possible. The doctors said it would be hard, but not impossible. To their shock and awe, it only took a few months, and Chandra was pregnant again. This time, she was determined to take it easy and protect the love that was growing inside of her. Damien was also very careful with Chandra and made sure she didn't do anything strenuous that would harm her or the baby. They decided to wait until she was at least four months before they would let anyone know that she was pregnant. And by that time, they would also be able to tell the sex of the baby. At their four-month ultrasound visit, Chandra and Damien found out they were carrying a baby boy. They were overjoyed at this thought. Chandra immediately called Aria and Aryanna to tell them the good news. They were both so happy to hear the joy in their sister's voice. Damien called his family as well. They were also overjoyed. They decided to start planning a visit right away. Granny Ann was overjoyed with the news and immediately called Grandpa Dan. Grandpa Dan wasn't feeling too well lately, so he and Granny Ann knew they wouldn't be able to take a trip any time soon. Clarissa and her new friend said they would love to visit again, but with all the work they were both doing at the church, they had to make the time.

It was a calm Sunday, and Chandra and Damien both had the day off and were sitting on the back deck, enjoying a nice glass of lemonade. This has been the only drink Chandra has been able to tolerate during this pregnancy. She was now seven months pregnant and felt as if she was as big as a house. Chandra was daydreaming when she was jolted back into reality by the telephone ringing. Damien ran inside to grab the phone. Immediately, Chandra could tell from the tone of his voice that something was wrong. She took the phone from Damien, and it was Granny Ann.

She said, "Baby girl, Grandpa Dan is not doing well and has asked to see you."

Chandra knew that if they were calling, she had to make it to Georgia soon. Grandpa Dan had been diagnosed with cancer and was now fighting for his life. Chandra called the hospital and put in time off for a visit back home. Her supervisors were more than accommodating. Chandra never called out or took time off, so they knew it must be an emergency. Damien asked around for other doctors to cover his upcoming shifts, and they gladly obliged. They were both blessed with amazing coworkers and an amazing work crew. Damien and Chandra loaded up their Tahoe and headed up north to Georgia. With everyone coming home, Chandra and Damien decided to stay at Granny Ann's home, knowing there would be absolutely no room at Clarissa's home. Aryanna and her husband were there as well as Aria and her husband.

When Chandra arrived at the home of Granny Ann, she immediately ran in the room to hug Grandpa Dan. He lit up at the sight of her. He hugged her and rubbed her belly. He didn't look sick at all. He just looks tired and old. She knew he was trying to put up a good look for her. He didn't want her worried about him. The entire day the women spent in the kitchen, cooking and catching up on each other's lives while the men stayed in the room with Grandpa Dan talked about sports. Grandpa Dan was a comedian about everything, so he had the men laughing all day. Aryanna and Aria were treating Chandra like she was delicate piece of fruit. They didn't want anything to happen to her while she was pregnant. She kept trying to reassure them that she was out of the woods, and their nephew was fine. They both kept making her sit down. While waiting on the food to finish cooking, the women would sit and talk about old times.

When the food was done, the women made their men's plates, and they all sat in the room with Grandpa Dan and laughed and sang. Clarissa had a voice of an angel, and Grandpa Dan loved to hear her sing. She was a shy singer, but her voice could make the angels smile. Dinner was amazing, and everyone was more than full after eating. Throughout the afternoon, many family members stopped by to see Grandpa Dan and to partake in the dinner the ladies had made. To go plates were walking out the door one by one. In their family, the ladies knew that everyone would come as soon as they heard food was being made. Their family was close like that. This had always been something that made Chandra happy. She adored her family and couldn't have prayed for a closer family with more love.

On the drive home, Chandra was sitting, smiling, and thinking of the wonderful time she had with her family. Grandpa Dan would start treatment this week and was very hopeful. Chandra and Damien were also hopeful and had faith that he would be okay. They had an amazing week with the family and couldn't wait to get home and rest. Being pregnant was starting to tire Chandra out really quick. The next few months flew by. Chandra was awakened in the middle of the night with pain. She felt as if someone was punching her in her stomach. She woke Damien and told him they needed to call everyone because she knew she was in labor. While Chandra took a shower and prepared for the trip to the hospital, Damien called both families. Clarissa, Granny Ann, and Aunt Josephine all got on the road to meet them at the hospital. They knew the baby would more than likely be born before they would make it, but they wanted to try to get there, anyways.

Chandra and Damien made it to the hospital, and Chandra was resting comfortably in the room. To their surprise, the family arrived at the hospital before the baby was born. Chandra was filled with love that they would come and be by her side. Chandra was in labor for hours. She managed to have her baby without medication. She was so happy. He was here. Chandra got a good look at her baby boy, and they took him off to wash him up and weigh him. Chandra started feeling dizzy and told her Aunt Josephine that something wasn't right. Aunt Josephine happened to look down and saw blood gushing from Chandra. Chandra heard the nurse and the doctor talking and the doctor told the family, "There's nothing more we can do. We can't stop the bleeding."

Chandra was hemorrhaging, and there was nothing they could do. Granny Ann and Aunt Josephine began praying. They knew that only God could fix it. They prayed and they prayed and by the grace of God, the bleeding subsided. The doctors had no answers for why Chandra didn't die, but everyone in that room knew that God did it. That same night, the family drove back to Georgia knowing that all was well with baby boy, Damien Jr and Chandra.

During their entire relationship, Damien has had his moments of cheating, verbal abuse, and selfishness. Chandra had taken this because the entire time she felt that she deserved everything he was giving her. During her pregnancy, Damien was mostly a loving and caring husband. He did go out with his friends and hung out all times of hours, and he did talk down to Chandra, but his fidelity was good. Chandra thought that was good enough. Everyday wasn't a bad day, and they did have some really good times. It was better than bad, and Chandra thought this was a great way to start. Once DJ was born, things seem to be going well. Damien worked a lot, so housework and baby duty was mainly on Chandra. But this was the deal since she had stopped working. Chandra was exhausted, but she knew that if she voiced it, there would be a huge argument, and she didn't want that. Damien was tired from working so many hours, and he would take it out on Chandra. She cried many days and nights to herself. After a while, Damien decided to allow Chandra to go home for a visit to get some rest and allow her family to help with DJ. She couldn't have been happier. She was able to go home and catch up on some much-needed rest and sleep.

When DJ was four months old, Damien and Chandra took a trip to Vermont to visit Damien's family. It was a great trip, and everyone fell in love with DJ. As soon as the trip was over, Damien let Chandra know that she would have to find a job. So when they returned to Florida, Chandra found a job in health care that would allow her to bring DJ to work with her. Chandra worked all types of hours, but she still managed to clean the house, take care of DJ, and make sure that all meals were cooked. Most of Chandra's money went into Damien, and he didn't mind spending it. He was still verbally abusing Chandra because he felt that she was beneath him and wasn't worthy of his love. In reality, he wasn't happy with himself. He would drink a lot and hang out with his friends. Chandra didn't mind because she was happier when he was out of the house.

It was a vicious cycle in their home. They would fight and Damien would make Chandra cry and put her down, and she would do more to try and please him. She was emotionally and physically exhausted. She knew in her heart that she deserved better, but her mind told her she didn't. All this time, Chandra would put up a front in front of both families because she didn't want anyone to know the way she was feeling inside. In the midst of it all, Chandra became pregnant with her second child. They waited until they were four months pregnant before telling anyone again. This time, they were pregnant with a baby girl. When Chandra was five months pregnant with her baby girl, tragedy struck. Grandpa Dan succumbed to his cancer. To her surprise, Damien agreed to take her home for the funeral. He loved to pretend in front of their families that he was doting and loving husband. While they were in Georgia, DJ cried to stay with Clarissa. Damien and Chandra agreed to let him stay for a few weeks, and they would come back and pick him up.

Damien and Chandra had been home for about a week, and Chandra was missing her baby boy. Damien was still working, and let Chandra know that he wouldn't be able to go with her to Georgia to pick up their baby boy. He decided to send Chandra on her own. She got in the car and drove off in the middle of night to go and pick up their baby boy. She was now six months pregnant. When she arrived in Georgia, she decided to stay a few weeks with family. She called Damien and to her surprise, he told her he didn't want her to return. He thought that it would be best if she got a doctor there and remain there for her pregnancy. She was hurt and shocked. It didn't hurt her as much as she thought it would, but it still hurt. Chandra was still calling and keeping Damien up to date on the status of their baby girl and letting him talk with DJ. Damien was always distant and acted as if he really didn't care about any of them. Damien was taking time off to visit his relatives and friends from home.

One night, Chandra woke up, call it women's intuition, but she was awake and she felt that something was off. She eventually fell back asleep and just ignored the feeling. The next day, she talked with Damien on the phone and found out that he was on vacation with some of his cousins. Chandra was close with her family, so this didn't seem strange to her at all. Chandra was sitting in her mom's room when she started going over the phone bill and noticed a number that she hadn't seen before. She noticed that this number was being called from her husband's phone at all times of the night. Chandra decided to call the number herself. A girl named Mary answered the phone.

Chandra asked, "Who is this, and what is your relationship to Damien?"

Mary answered, "My name is Mary, and Damien and I are friends getting to know each other better. Who is this?"

Chandra replied, "I thought I was his wife."

Mary said, "That has nothing to do with me, and you should know that we are sleeping together."

Chandra hung up the phone and couldn't believe what she had just heard. She was pregnant with his child, and he could still do this to her. Chandra's heart was broken. Not again, how could she continue to do this with him. He obviously didn't want her or her children in his life. She took her time and called Damien to talk with him. He denied sleeping with Mary, but also didn't apologize for it. It was what it was, and Chandra could take it or leave it. He also told Chandra that he didn't want her to come to visit him and his parent's house, and when he wanted to see the kids, he would let her know. Baby girl wasn't even born yet, and he had already dismissed her from his life. He didn't care about anyone but himself, and Chandra was coming to the realization. Once again after a few months of talking and Chandra begging to come home, Damien allowed her to come home. She showed up, and Damien acted as if the last few months hadn't happened, and to avoid the drama, Chandra played along. Damien took Chandra to visit Vermont. She was nine months pregnant and went into labor during the visit. Chandra ended up having the baby in Vermont, and she ended up staying in Vermont with Damien's family for about a month before he came back to pick her, DJ, and baby girl, Alexa, up. He said he was working, but Chandra didn't trust him. She didn't say anything as usual, but she knew in her heart that he was cheating again. At this time, she didn't have the time or the energy to find out with who.

Chandra spent the next few years taking care of their children and taking care of their home. She was moving on autopilot. She knew that every day that Damien came home, he would have another complaint about her. She began putting on weight, and that was a major problem in their home. Damien was drinking when he wasn't working. Out of the blue, Damien began going to the gym more and more. Chandra chose to ignore that as well until one day Chandra was at the park with DJ and Alexa, and her phone rang.

She answered to some woman telling her that she had been sleeping with Damien, and she was pregnant with his child. To her shock, Chandra wasn't surprised or hurt. It was at the point in her life to where she was numb to all that was going on around her. She was cooking and cleaning and trying to be the best mother she could be. She knew that all she was to Damien was a maid and a sex toy when he wanted to use it. Damien was walking around the house like he was disgusted and angry all the time. He was great at pretending. When they were in front of people of family, Damien was the perfect husband and father. Absolutely no one knew the pain and the heartache Chandra truly felt. There were many days the only thing that kept her alive was her children. They needed her, and there was no way she was going to purposefully leave them alone in this world with this man.

When Damien came home from work, Chandra confronted him about the phone call that she had received. He didn't deny it. He took the time to explain to Chandra that the woman was a good friend, and it just happened. He was praising the woman, and Chandra couldn't understand why he wasn't more hurt, or why he didn't even pretend to care about her heart. What had she done so wrong to him, for him to hate her the way that he did? Damien told Chandra that he would end it. He said that he would call off the relationship. Chandra didn't care about him calling off the relationship at this point. All she wanted was revenge. How dare he keep hurting her in this way? How many times could she blame herself for the actions of this man? Did she want her kids to grow up and think this was love? These are all answers that she needed to answer for herself. She knew that she was done. She couldn't do this anymore. She wanted him to know the hurt that she had felt for all the years prior. Chandra found a babysitter and went out and had her a wild night of fun. It didn't make her feel any better. It made her feel so horrible. She knew that this was not who she was and couldn't believe that she had allowed him to turn her into that person. Chandra vowed to never go out there again. She felt dirty and used.

When Chandra returned home, Damien was there wanting to talk with her. She agreed to talk with him. He decided that he wanted their marriage to work, and he would do anything to make it work. This was the first time that he had showed any concern or any signs that he wanted this relationship at all. It was almost real to Chandra. She almost believed him. Damien and Chandra decided together they would work on their relationship together. That afternoon, they took a walk around their neighborhood with their kids. As they were walking, they noticed there were signs posted on all the mailboxes in the area. They were signs about a local church in the area. Chandra had grown up serving God her entire life, but Damien wasn't a part of any church. Chandra took one of the flyers and asked Damien to join her in attending this church that was advertised. He agreed. He knew that if he said no, there was a possibility that Chandra would leave him.

Sunday morning came, and Chandra got dressed for morning service. She and Damien were both nervous because even though Chandra was rooted in God, she had backslid and hadn't truly served him in years. She knew that her life had taken on its on highway, and God hadn't been driving the vehicle. Damien's family were Catholic, so he didn't know what to expect. There were a few times that he had attended services with Chandra in the past when she would want to go which wasn't a lot at all. They were the "holiday" services that she felt was necessary to attend. Everyone was dressed and ready to go. Chandra had gained a bit of weight, so she wore her maternity dress, and the kids were dressed up so nice. Damien had worn the only suit he owned which was usually only worn at funerals. They made it to the church and walked in. The usher had the audacity to seat them in the front of the church. Chandra was still very much upset at Damien but kept telling herself that she was going to try.

As the pastor began to preach, Chandra looked over and saw that Damien was fixated on every word the man was saying. She asked herself was this all an act. She wanted to believe that he wanted to change, but the biggest part of her didn't want to be fooled again. At the end of service when the pastor called for men and women to repent and give their lives to God, Chandra saw Damien put his hand up and walked up front and bowed his knee. She couldn't believe what had just happened. What in the world was he doing?

He was indeed taking this too far. She knew that he must be faking. God would never call on a man like him. She was too angry to remember that the God she once served forgave her of all that she had done. Chandra watched the tears flow from Damien's face and saw the members gather around and hug him. She felt sorry for him, but she couldn't allow herself to give in to those feelings just yet.

A few weeks had passed, and Damien and Chandra and the kids were regularly attending church services and taking the time to also get to know a few of its regular attendees. They seemed like good people, but Chandra was still guarded. She and Damien had also been attending some regular counseling sessions with the pastor that were going pretty well. They still had their arguments, and the past still haunted them, but they both were putting all their efforts in to making this marriage work. They both had concluded that the only thing that would save them and their marriage was the love and the forgiveness of God. After about a month, Chandra gave her life to Christ as well. They were moving forward, and God was moving in them and their lives. Granny Ann couldn't have been happier about their decision to serve God. This was something she had dreamed about for so long. She was a prayer warrior and knew that God had to come and change them both before their marriage would ever work. After the pain and the forgiveness, Chandra found out that she was pregnant again. She and Damien couldn't have been happier about their upcoming arrival.

ABOUT THE AUTHOR

T. Pelletier is a USAF veteran and currently married to a military member. She and her husband have been married for twenty years. They have three amazing children. She grew up in the south, and my husband grew up in the north. Having their lives intertwined is very entertaining. They grew up in two different worlds. Writing this book was almost therapeutic. Repenting and giving their lives to Christ has been the best decision they ever made, and it made them into who they are today.